_To_

From

Date

365 daily devotions

A WOMAN OF FAITH

The quoted ideas expressed in this book (but not Scripture verses) are not, in all cases, exact quotations, as some have been edited for clarity and brevity. In all cases, the author has attempted to maintain the speaker's original intent. In some cases, quoted material for this book was obtained from secondary sources, primarily print media. While every effort was made to ensure the accuracy of these sources, the accuracy cannot be guaranteed. For additions, deletions, corrections, or clarifications in future editions of this text, please write Freeman-Smith, LLC.

Scripture quotations are taken from:

Scriptures marked NIV® are from the Holy Bible, New International Version®. Copyright © 1973, 1978, 1984 by International Bible Society. Used by permission of Zondervan Publishing House. All rights reserved.

Scriptures marked NASB are taken from the New American Standard Bible®. © Copyright The Lockman Foundation 1960, 1962, 1963, 1968, 1971, 1972, 1973, 1975, 1977, 1995. Used by permission. (www.Lockman.org).

Scriptures marked NKJV are taken from the New King James Version®. Copyright © 1982 by Thomas Nelson, Inc. Used by permission. All rights reserved.

Scriptures marked NLT are taken from the Holy Bible, New Living Translation, copyright © 1996. Used by permission of Tyndale House Publishers, Inc., Wheaton, Illinois 60189. All rights reserved.

Scriptures marked NCV are quoted from The Holy Bible, New Century Version, copyright © 1987, 1988, 1991 by Word Publishing, Nashville, TN 37214. Used by permission.

Scriptures marked KJV are taken from the King James Version.

Scripture quotations marked MSG are taken from The Message. Copyright © by Eugene H. Peterson 1993, 1994, 1995. Used by permission of NavPress Publishing Group.

Scripture quotations marked ICB are taken from the International Children's Bible, New Century Version © 1986, 1988 by Word Publishing, Nashville, TN 37214. Used by permission.

Scripture quotations marked TLB are taken from The Living Bible copyright © 1971. Used by permission of Tyndale House Publishers, Inc., Wheaton, Illinois 60189. All rights reserved.

Scripture quotations marked HCSB are taken from the Holman Christian Standard Bible ®, Copyright © 1999, 2000, 2002, 2003 by Holman Bible Publishers. Used by permission. Holman Christian Standard Bible®, Holman CSB®, and HCSB® are federally registered trademarks of Holman Bible Publishers.

Cover Design by Kim Russell / Wahoo Designs
Page Layout by Bart Dawson

ISBN 978-1-58334-505-4

Printed in the United States of America

365 daily devotions

A
WOMAN
OF
FAITH

Introduction

In today's world, being a woman of faith can be a daunting task. Never have expectations been higher, never have distractions been so plentiful, and never have demands been greater. Thankfully, God stands ready, willing, and able to help you in every facet of your life if you ask Him. But it's important to remember that the best way to ask God for His wisdom and His strength is to ask Him often.

God's promises are eternal and unchanging. But, as every woman knows, life in today's fast-paced world can be so confusing that it becomes easy to lose sight, at least temporarily, of God's blessings and His mercy. The ideas in this book serve as a reminder of the joy and the abundance that God offers to all believers who place their faith in Him.

The fabric of daily life is woven together with the threads of habit, and no habit is more important than that of consistent prayer and daily devotion to our Creator. And this book is intended to help. This text contains 365 chapters, one for each day of the year. During the next 12 months, please try this experiment: read a chapter each day. If you're already committed to a daily worship time, this book will enrich that experience. If you are not, the simple act of giving God a few minutes each morning will change the direction and the quality of your life.

This text addresses topics of particular interest to you, a Christian woman living in an uncertain world. If you take the time to meditate upon these devotional readings, you will be reminded of God's love, of His Son, and of His promises. May these pages be a blessing to you, and may you, in turn, be a blessing to those whom God has seen fit to place along your path.

A Woman of Faith

*I tell you the truth, if you have faith and do not doubt...
you can say to this mountain "Go and throw yourself into
the sea," and it will be done.*

MATTHEW 21:21 NIV

You live in difficult times, times when your faith is tested every day by the distractions and temptations of 21st-century life. As you witness suffering around the world—and suffering right here at home—you may have questions that defy easy answers. But even during life's darkest days, you must trust God to protect you now and throughout eternity.

Are you a woman of faith? Are you the kind of woman who embraces God's love even when she can't understand God's plan? And have you allowed God's only begotten Son to reign over your heart and your life? If so, then the Creator of the universe stands ready, willing, and able to solve every single one of your problems. Your job, of course, is to let Him.

Faith in faith is pointless. Faith in a living, active God moves mountains.

BETH MOORE

He Heals the Brokenhearted

God blesses the people who patiently endure testing. Afterward they will receive the crown of life that God has promised to those who love him.

JAMES 1:12 NLT

Women of every generation have experienced adversity, and this generation is no different. But, today's women face challenges that previous generations could have scarcely imagined. Thankfully, although the world continues to change, God's love remains constant. And, He remains ready to comfort us and strengthen us whenever we turn to Him.

Psalm 147 promises, "He heals the brokenhearted, and binds their wounds" (v. 3). When we are troubled, we must call upon God, and, in His own time and according to His own plan, He will heal us.

If you are like most women, it is simply a fact of life: from time to time, you worry. You worry about health, about finances, about safety, about relationships, about family, and about countless other challenges of life, some great and some small. Where is the best place to take your worries? Take them to God. Take your troubles to Him, and your fears, and your sorrows. Seek protection from the One who cannot be moved.

Living Righteously

But now you must be holy in everything you do, just as God—who chose you to be his children—is holy. For he himself has said, "You must be holy because I am holy."
1 PETER 1:15-16 NLT

When we seek righteousness in our own lives— and when we seek the companionship of those who do likewise—we reap the spiritual rewards that God intends for us to enjoy. When we behave ourselves as godly men and women, we honor God. When we live righteously and according to God's commandments, He blesses us in ways that we cannot fully understand.

Today, as you fulfill your responsibilities, hold fast to that which is good, and associate yourself with believers who behave themselves in like fashion. When you do, your good works will serve as a powerful example for others and as a worthy offering to your Creator.

Do nothing that you would not like to be doing when Jesus comes. Go no place where you would not like to be found when He returns.

CORRIE TEN BOOM

Giving Thanks to the Giver

Is anyone happy? Let him sing songs of praise.

JAMES 5:13 NIV

The 100th Psalm reminds us that the entire earth should "Shout for joy to the Lord." As God's children, we are blessed beyond measure, but sometimes, as busy women living in a demanding world, we are slow to count our gifts and even slower to give thanks to the Giver.

Our blessings include life and health, family and friends, freedom and possessions—for starters. And, the gifts we receive from God are multiplied when we share them. May we always give thanks to God for His blessings, and may we always demonstrate our gratitude by sharing our gifts with others.

Trusting God does not make me less of a woman. It doesn't compromise my personality as a strong woman. Depending on Him celebrates the wonderful, miraculous gift He has entrusted to me. Trusting Him is my strength.

SUZANNE DALE EZELL

Joy is faith feasting and celebrating the One in Whom it trusts.

SUSAN LENZKES

Comforting Others

Blessed be the God and Father of our Lord Jesus Christ, the Father of mercies and the God of all comfort. He comforts us in all our affliction, so that we may be able to comfort those who are in any kind of affliction, through the comfort we ourselves receive from God.

2 CORINTHIANS 1:3-4 HCSB

The 118th Psalm reminds us, "This is the day which the Lord hath made; we will rejoice and be glad in it" (v. 24 KJV). As we rejoice in this day that the Lord has given us, let us remember that an important part of today's celebration is the time we spend comforting those in need.

Each day provides countless opportunities to encourage others and to assist those who need our help. When we do, we spread seeds of hope and happiness.

Today, when you encounter someone who needs a helping hand or a comforting word, be generous with both. You possess the power to make the world a better place one person—and one hug—at a time. When you use that power wisely, you make your own corner of the world a kinder, gentler, happier place.

Solving Life's Riddles

But the wisdom from above is first pure, then peace-loving, gentle, compliant, full of mercy and good fruits, without favoritism and hypocrisy.

JAMES 3:17 HCSB

Life presents each of us with countless questions, conundrums, doubts, and problems. Thankfully, the riddles of everyday living are not too difficult to solve if we look for answers in the right places. When we have questions, we should consult God's Word, we should seek the guidance of the Holy Spirit, and we should trust the counsel of God-fearing friends and family members.

Are you facing a difficult decision? Take your concerns to God and avail yourself of the messages and mentors that He has placed along your path. When you do, God will speak to you in His own way and in His own time, and when He does, you can most certainly trust the answers that He gives.

We need to be able to make decisions based on what we know rather than on what we feel.

JOYCE MEYER

Your Great Expectations

When dreams come true, there is life and joy.

PROVERBS 13:12 NLT

Do you expect your future to be bright? Are you willing to dream king-sized dreams . . . and are you willing to work diligently to make those dreams happen? Hopefully so—after all, God promises that we can do "all things" through Him. Yet most of us, even the most devout among us, live far below our potential. We take half measures; we dream small dreams; we waste precious time and energy on the distractions of the world. But God has other plans for us.

Our Creator intends that we live faithfully, hopefully, courageously, and abundantly. He knows that we are capable of so much more; and He wants us to do the things we're capable of doing; and He wants us to begin doing those things today.

Allow your dreams a place in your prayers and plans. God-given dreams can help you move into the future He is preparing for you.

BARBARA JOHNSON

Faith That Works

For in the gospel a righteousness from God is revealed, a righteousness that is by faith from first to last, just as it is written: "The righteous will live by faith."

ROMANS 1:17 NIV

Through every stage of your life, God stands by your side, ready to strengthen you and protect you . . . if you have faith in Him. When you place your faith, your trust, indeed your life in the hands of Christ Jesus, you'll be amazed at the marvelous things He can do with you and through you.

So make this promise to yourself and keep it: make certain that your faith is a faith that works. How? You can strengthen your faith through praise, through worship, through Bible study, and through prayer. When you do so, you'll learn to trust God's plans. With Him, all things are possible, and He stands ready to open a world of possibilities to you . . . if you have faith.

If you allow circumstances to effect your service and commitment to Him, then you are walking by feelings and not by faith.

ANONYMOUS

Finding Fulfillment

You haven't done this before. Ask, using my name, and you will receive, and you will have abundant joy.

JOHN 16:24 NLT

Everywhere we turn, or so it seems, the world promises fulfillment, contentment, and happiness. But the contentment that the world offers is fleeting and incomplete. Thankfully, the fulfillment that God offers is all encompassing and everlasting.

Happiness depends less upon our circumstances than our thoughts. When we turn our thoughts to God, to His gifts, and to His glorious creation, we experience the joy that God intends for His children. But, when we focus on the negative aspects of life—or when we disobey God's commandments—we cause ourselves needless suffering.

Sometimes, amid the inevitable hustle and bustle of daily life, we can forfeit—albeit temporarily—the joy of Christ as we wrestle with the challenges of daily living. Yet God's Word is clear: fulfillment through Christ is available to all who seek it and claim it. Count yourself among that number. Seek first a personal, transforming relationship with Jesus, and then claim the joy, the fulfillment, and the spiritual abundance that the Shepherd offers His sheep.

God's Attentiveness

For the eyes of the Lord range throughout the earth to show Himself strong for those whose hearts are completely His.

2 CHRONICLES 16:9 HCSB

God is not distant, and He is not disinterested. To the contrary, your Heavenly Father is attentive to your needs. In fact, God knows precisely what you need and when you need it. But, He still wants to talk with you, and if you're a faithful believer, you should want to talk to Him, too.

Jesus made it clear to His disciples: they should pray always. And so should we. Genuine, heartfelt prayer changes things and it changes us. When we lift our hearts to our Father in heaven, we open ourselves to a never-ending source of divine wisdom and infinite love.

Do you have questions that you simply can't answer? Ask for the guidance of your Creator. Do you sincerely seek the gift of everlasting love and eternal life? Accept the grace of God's only begotten Son. Whatever your need, no matter how great or small, pray about it. Instead of waiting for mealtimes or bedtimes, follow the instruction of your Savior: pray always and never lose heart. And remember: God is not just near; He is here, and He's ready to talk with you. Now!

Embraced by God

The unfailing love of the Lord never ends!
LAMENTATIONS 3:22 NLT

Every day of your life—indeed, every moment of your life—you are embraced by God. He is always with you, and His love for you is deeper and more profound than you can imagine. And now, precisely because you are a wondrous creation treasured by God, a question presents itself: What will you do in response to God's love? Will you ignore it or return it? Will you return it or neglect it? The decision, of course, is yours and yours alone.

When you open yourself to God's love, you feel differently about yourself, your neighbors, and your world. When you embrace God's love, you share His message and you obey His commandments.

When you accept the Father's grace and share His love, you are blessed here on earth and throughout all eternity. Accept His love today.

Love is not something God does; love is something God is.

BETH MOORE

His Strength

The Lord is the strength of my life.

PSALM 27:1 KJV

Have you made God the cornerstone of your life, or is He relegated to a few hours on Sunday morning? Have you genuinely allowed God to reign over every corner of your heart, or have you attempted to place Him in a spiritual compartment? The answer to these questions will determine the direction of your day and your life.

God loves you. In times of trouble, He will comfort you; in times of sorrow, He will dry your tears. When you are or weak or sorrowful, God is as near as your next breath. He stands at the door of your heart and waits. Welcome Him in and allow Him to rule. And then, accept the peace, and the strength, and the protection, and the abundance that only God can give.

So rejoice! You are giving Him what He asks you to give Him—the chance to show you what He can do.

AMY CARMICHAEL

Still Growing

When I was a child, I spoke and thought and reasoned as a child does. But when I grew up, I put away childish things.

1 CORINTHIANS 13:11 NLT

If we are to grow as women, we need both knowledge and wisdom. Knowledge is found in textbooks. Wisdom, on the other hand, is found through experience, through years of trial and error, and through careful attention to the Word of God. Knowledge is an important building block in a well-lived life, and it pays rich dividends both personally and professionally. But, wisdom is even more important because it refashions not only our minds, but also our hearts.

When it comes to your faith, God doesn't intend for you to stand still. He wants you to keep growing as a woman and as a spiritual being. No matter how "grown-up" you may be, you still have growing to do. And the more you grow, the more beautiful you become, inside and out.

Growing in any area of the Christian life takes time, and the key is daily sitting at the feet of Jesus.

CYNTHIA HEALD

Joy Is . . .

Rejoice evermore. Pray without ceasing. In every thing give thanks: for this is the will of God in Christ Jesus concerning you.

1 Thessalonians 5:16-18 KJV

The Lord made it clear: He intended that His joy would become their joy. And it still holds true today: The Lord intends that His believers share His love with His joy in their hearts.

Mother Teresa once said, "Joy is the characteristic by which God uses us to re-make the distressing into the desired, the discarded into the creative. Joy is prayer . . . Joy is strength . . . Joy is love . . . Joy is a net of love by which you can catch souls."

If, today, your heart is heavy, open the door of your soul to Christ. He will give you peace and joy. And if you already have the joy of Christ in your heart, share it freely, just as Christ freely shared His joy with you.

Joy is a by-product not of happy circumstances, education or talent, but of a healthy relationship with God and a determination to love Him no matter what.

Barbara Johnson

And the Greatest of These

Love is patient, love is kind and is not jealous; love does not brag and is not arrogant, does not act unbecomingly; it does not seek its own, is not provoked, does not take into account a wrong suffered, does not rejoice in unrighteousness, but rejoices with the truth; bears all things, believes all things, hopes all things, endures all things.

1 CORINTHIANS 13:4-7 NASB

The beautiful words of 1st Corinthians 13 remind us that love is God's commandment: "But now abide faith, hope, love, these three; but the greatest of these is love" (v. 13, NASB). Faith is important, of course. So, too, is hope. But, love is more important still. Christ showed His love for us on the cross, and, as Christians, we are called upon to return Christ's love by sharing it. Today, let us spread Christ's love to families, friends, and strangers by word and by deed.

The reason why God's servants love creatures so much is that they see how much Christ loves them, and it is one of the properties of love to love what is loved by the person we love.

ST. CATHERINE OF SIENA

The Donut and the Hole

Be careful what you think, because your thoughts run your life.

PROVERBS 4:23 NCV

On the wall of a little donut shop, the sign said: As you travel through life, brother, Whatever be your goal, Keep your eye upon the donut, And not upon the hole.

Are you a Christian who keeps your eye upon the donut, or have you acquired the bad habit of looking only at the hole? Hopefully, you spend most of your waking hours looking at the donut (and thanking God for it).

Christianity and pessimism don't mix. So do yourself a favor: choose to be a hope-filled Christian. Think optimistically about your life and your future. Trust your hopes, not your fears. Take time to celebrate God's glorious creation. And then, when you've filled your heart with hope and gladness, share your optimism with your friends. They'll be better for it, and so will you. But not necessarily in that order.

A pessimist is someone who believes that when her cup runneth over she'll need a mop.

BARBARA JOHNSON

Perseverance and Purpose

Let us not become weary in doing good, for at the proper time we will reap a harvest if we do not give up.

GALATIANS 6:9 NIV

As you continue to seek God's purpose for your life, you will undoubtedly experience your fair share of disappointments, detours, false starts, and failures. When you do, don't become discouraged: God's not finished with you yet.

The old saying is as true today as it was when it was first spoken: "Life is a marathon, not a sprint." That's why wise travelers select a traveling companion who never tires and never falters. That partner, of course, is your Heavenly Father.

Are you tired? Ask God for strength. Are you discouraged? Believe in His promises. Are you defeated? Pray as if everything depended upon God, and work as if everything depended upon you. And finally, have faith that you play an important role in God's great plan for mankind—because you do.

He Persevered and so Must We

If you do nothing in a difficult time, your strength is limited.

PROVERBS 24:10 HCSB

In a world filled with roadblocks and stumbling blocks, we need strength, courage, and perseverance. And, as an example of perfect perseverance, we need look no further than our Savior, Jesus Christ.

Jesus finished what He began. Despite the torture He endured, despite the shame of the cross, Jesus was steadfast in His faithfulness to God. We, too, must remain faithful, especially during times of hardship.

Perhaps you are in a hurry for God to reveal His plans for your life. If so, be forewarned: God operates on His own timetable, not yours. Sometimes, God may answer your prayers with silence, and when He does, you must patiently persevere. In times of trouble, you must remain steadfast and trust in the merciful goodness of your Heavenly Father. Whatever your problem, He can handle it. Your job is to keep persevering until He does.

If we stay with the Lord, enduring to the end of His great plan for us, we will enjoy the rest that results from living in the kingdom of God.

SERITA ANN JAKES

Prayer Now

Rejoice in hope; be patient in affliction; be persistent in prayer.

ROMANS 12:12 HCSB

Prayer is a powerful tool for communicating with our Creator; it is an opportunity to commune with the Giver of all things good. Prayer is not a thing to be taken lightly or to be used infrequently. Prayer should never be reserved for mealtimes or for bedtimes; it should be an ever-present focus in our daily lives.

In his first letter to the Thessalonians, Paul wrote, "Rejoice evermore. Pray without ceasing. In every thing give thanks: for this is the will of God in Christ Jesus concerning you" (v. 5:17-18 KJV). Paul's words apply to every Christian of every generation.

Today, instead of turning things over in our minds, let us turn them over to God in prayer. Instead of worrying about our decisions, let's trust God to help us make them. Today, let us pray constantly about things great and small. God is listening, and He wants to hear from us. Now.

Pray as if it's all up to God, work as if it's all up to you.

ANONYMOUS

Living on Purpose

It is God who works in you to will and to act according to his good purpose.

PHILIPPIANS 2:13 NIV

Life is best lived on purpose. And purpose, like everything else in the universe, begins with God. Whether you realize it or not, God has a plan for your life, a divine calling, a direction in which He is leading you. When you welcome God into your heart and establish a genuine relationship with Him, He will begin, in time, to make His purposes known.

Sometimes, God's intentions will be clear to you; other times, God's plan will seem uncertain at best. But even on those difficult days when you are unsure which way to turn, you must never lose sight of these overriding facts: God created you for a reason; He has important work for you to do; and He's waiting patiently for you to do it.

And the next step is up to you.

Victory is the result of Christ's life lived out in the believer. It is important to see that victory, not defeat, is God's purpose for His children.

CORRIE TEN BOOM

His Answer to Our Guilt

If My people who are called by My name will humble themselves, and pray and seek My face, and turn from their wicked ways, then I will hear from heaven, and will forgive their sin and heal their land.

2 Chronicles 7:14 NKJV

All of us have sinned. Sometimes our sins result from our own stubborn rebellion against God's commandments. And sometimes, we are swept up in events that are beyond our abilities to control. Under either set of circumstances, we may experience intense feelings of guilt. But God has an answer for the guilt that we feel. That answer, of course, is His forgiveness. When we confess our wrongdoings and repent from them, we are forgiven by the One who created us.

Are you troubled by feelings of guilt or regret? If so, you must repent from your misdeeds, and you must ask your Heavenly Father for His forgiveness. When you do so, He will forgive you completely and without reservation. Then, you must forgive yourself just as God has forgiven you: thoroughly and unconditionally.

Your Own Worst Critic?

A devout life does bring wealth, but it's the rich simplicity of being yourself before God.

1 TIMOTHY 6:6 MSG

Are you your own worst critic? If so, it's time to become a little more understanding of the woman you see whenever you look into the mirror.

Millions of words have been written about various ways to improve self-image and increase self-esteem. Yet, maintaining a healthy self-image is, to a surprising extent, a matter of doing three things: 1. behaving ourselves 2. thinking healthy thoughts 3. finding a purpose for your life that pleases your Creator and yourself.

The Bible affirms the importance of self-acceptance by teaching Christians to love others as they love themselves (Matthew 22:37-40). God accepts us just as we are. And, if He accepts us—faults and all—then who are we to believe otherwise?

Being loved by Him whose opinion matters most gives us the security to risk loving, too—even loving ourselves.

GLORIA GAITHER

Stillness

Be still, and know that I am God....

PSALM 46:10 KJV

Are you so busy that you rush through the day with scarcely a single moment for quiet contemplation and prayer? If so, it's time to reorder your priorities.

We live in a noisy world, a world filled with distractions, frustrations, and complications. But if we allow the distractions of a clamorous world to separate us from God's peace, we do ourselves a profound disservice. If we are to maintain righteous minds and compassionate hearts, we must take time each day for prayer and for meditation. We must make ourselves still in the presence of our Creator. We must quiet our minds and our hearts so that we might sense God's will, God's love, and God's Son.

Has the busy pace of life robbed you of the peace that might otherwise be yours through Jesus Christ? Nothing is more important than the time you spend with your Savior. So be still and claim the inner peace that is your spiritual birthright: the peace of Jesus Christ. It is offered freely; it has been paid for in full; it is yours for the asking. So ask. And then share.

Busy with Our Thoughts

People's thoughts can be like a deep well, but someone with understanding can find the wisdom there.

PROVERBS 20:5 NCV

Because we are human, we are always busy with our thoughts. We simply can't help ourselves. Our brains never shut off, and even while we're sleeping, we mull things over in our minds. The question is not if we will think; the question is how will we think and what will we think about.

Today, focus your thoughts on God and His will. And if you've been plagued by pessimism and doubt, stop thinking like that! Place your faith in God and give thanks for His blessings. Think optimistically about your world and your life. It's the wise way to use your mind. And besides, since you will always be busy with your thoughts, you might as well make those thoughts pleasing (to God) and helpful (to you and yours).

The things we think are the things that feed our souls. If we think on pure and lovely things, we shall grow pure and lovely like them; and the converse is equally true.

HANNAH WHITALL SMITH

Accepting His Will

Should we accept only good from God and not adversity?
JOB 2:10 HCSB

All of us must, from time to time, endure days filled with suffering and pain. And as human beings with limited understanding, we can never fully understand the plans of our Father in Heaven. But as believers in a benevolent God, we must always trust Him.

When Jesus went to the Mount of Olives, He poured out His heart to God (Luke 22). Jesus knew of the agony that He was destined to endure, but He also knew that God's will must be done.

We, like our Savior, face trials that bring fear and trembling to the very depths of our souls, but like Christ, we, too, must seek God's will, not our own. When we learn to accept God's will without reservation, we experience the peace that He offers to wise believers who trust Him completely.

Surrender to the Lord is not a tremendous sacrifice, not an agonizing performance. It is the most sensible thing you can do.

CORRIE TEN BOOM

Talking to the Father

You do not have because you do not ask.

JAMES 4:2 HCSB

Sometimes, amid the demands and the frustrations of everyday life, we forget to slow ourselves down long enough to talk with God. Instead of turning our thoughts and prayers to Him, we rely upon our own resources. Instead of praying for strength and courage, we seek to manufacture it within ourselves. Instead of asking God for guidance, we depend only upon our own limited wisdom. The results of such behaviors are unfortunate and, on occasion, tragic.

Are you in need? Ask God to sustain you. Are you troubled? Take your worries to Him in prayer. Are you weary? Seek God's strength. In all things great and small, seek God's wisdom and His grace. He hears your prayers, and He will answer. All you must do is ask.

When you ask God to do something, don't ask timidly; put your whole heart into it.

MARIE T. FREEMAN

Beyond Bitterness

All bitterness, anger and wrath, insult and slander must be removed from you, along with all wickedness. And be kind and compassionate to one another, forgiving one another, just as God also forgave you in Christ.

EPHESIANS 4:31-32 HCSB

Are you mired in the quicksand of bitterness or regret? If so, you are not only disobeying God's Word, you are also wasting your time. The world holds few if any rewards for those who remain angrily focused upon the past. Still, the act of forgiveness is difficult for all but the most saintly men and women.

Being frail, fallible, imperfect human beings, most of us are quick to anger, quick to blame, slow to forgive, and even slower to forget. Yet as Christians, we are commanded to forgive others, just as we, too, have been forgiven.

If there exists even one person—alive or dead—against whom you hold bitter feelings, it's time to forgive. Or, if you are embittered against yourself for some past mistake or shortcoming, it's finally time to forgive yourself and move on. Hatred, bitterness, and regret are not part of God's plan for your life. Forgiveness is.

The Gift of Cheerfulness

A miserable heart means a miserable life; a cheerful heart fills the day with a song.

PROVERBS 15:15 MSG

Cheerfulness is a gift that we give to others and to ourselves. And, as believers who have been saved by a risen Christ, why shouldn't we be cheerful? The answer, of course, is that we have every reason to honor our Savior with joy in our hearts, smiles on our faces, and words of celebration on our lips.

Few things in life are more sad, or, for that matter, more absurd, than grumpy Christians. Christ promises us lives of abundance and joy if we accept His love and His grace. Yet sometimes, even the most righteous among us are beset by fits of ill temper and frustration. During these moments, we may not feel like turning our thoughts and prayers to Christ, but if we seek to gain perspective and peace, that's precisely what we must do.

Are you a cheerful Christian? You should be! And what is the best way to attain the joy that is rightfully yours? By giving Christ what is rightfully His: your heart, your soul, and your life.

Beyond Discouragement

The Lord is my light and my salvation; whom shall I fear? The Lord is the strength of my life; of whom shall I be afraid?

PSALM 27:1 NKJV

Life can be difficult and discouraging at times. During our darkest moments, we can depend upon our friends and family, and upon God. When we do, we find the courage to face even the darkest days with hopeful hearts and willing hands.

Eleanor Roosevelt advised, "You gain strength, courage, and confidence by every great experience in which you really stop to look fear in the face. You are able to say to yourself, 'I lived through this horror. I can take the next thing that comes along.' You must do the thing you think you cannot do."

So the next time you find your courage tested to the limit, remember that you're probably stronger than you think. And remember—with you, your friends, your family and your God all working together, you have nothing to fear.

Discipline Matters

I discipline my body and bring it under strict control, so that after preaching to others, I myself will not be disqualified.

1 CORINTHIANS 9:27 HCSB

God's Word is clear: as believers, we are called to lead lives of discipline, diligence, moderation, and maturity. But the world often tempts us to behave otherwise. Everywhere we turn, or so it seems, we are faced with powerful temptations to behave in undisciplined, ungodly ways.

We live in a world in which leisure is glorified and misbehavior is glamorized. But God has other plans. He did not create us for lives of mischief or mediocrity; He created us for far greater things.

Life's greatest rewards seldom fall into our laps; to the contrary, God rewards diligence and righteousness just as certainly as He punishes laziness and sin. As believers in a just God, we should behave accordingly.

If I could just hang in there, being faithful to my own tasks, God would make me joyful and content. The responsibility is mine, but the power is His.

PEG RANKIN

Beyond Envy

Let us not become boastful, challenging one another, envying one another.

GALATIANS 5:26 NASB

Because we are frail, imperfect human beings, we are sometimes envious of others. But God's Word warns us that envy is sin. Thus, we must guard ourselves against the natural tendency to feel resentment and jealousy when other people experience good fortune.

As believers, we have absolutely no reason to be envious of any people on earth. After all, as Christians we are already recipients of the greatest gift in all creation: God's grace. We have been promised the gift of eternal life through God's only begotten Son, and we must count that gift as our most precious possession.

Rather than succumbing to the sin of envy, we should focus on the marvelous things that God has done for us. So here's a surefire formula for a happier, healthier life: Count your own blessings and let your neighbors counts theirs. It's the godly way to live.

Discontent dries up the soul.

ELISABETH ELLIOT

Forgiveness Is a Form of Wisdom

People with good sense restrain their anger; they earn esteem by overlooking wrongs.

PROVERBS 19:11 NLT

Genuine love is an exercise in forgiveness. If we wish to build lasting relationships, we must learn how to forgive. Why? Because our loved ones are imperfect (as are we). How often must we forgive our family and friends? More times than we can count. Why? Because that's what God wants us to do.

Perhaps granting forgiveness is hard for you. If so, you are not alone. Genuine, lasting forgiveness is often difficult to achieve—difficult but not impossible. Thankfully, with God's help, all things are possible, and that includes forgiveness. But, even though God is willing to help, He expects you to do some of the work. And make no mistake: forgiveness is work, which is okay with God. He knows that the payoffs are worth the effort.

Doing an injury puts you below your enemy; revenging an injury makes you even with him; forgiving an injury sets you above him!

ANONYMOUS

God First

Honor GOD with everything you own; give him the first and the best. Your barns will burst, your wine vats will brim over.

PROVERBS 3:9-10 MSG

As you think about the nature of your relationship with God, remember this: you will always have some type of relationship with Him—it is inevitable that your life must be lived in relationship to God. The question is not if you will have a relationship with Him; the burning question is whether or not that relationship will be one that seeks to honor Him . . . or not.

Are you willing to place God first in your life? And, are you willing to welcome God's Son into your heart? Unless you can honestly answer these questions with a resounding yes, then your relationship with God isn't what it could be or should be. Thankfully, God is always available, He's always ready to forgive, and He's waiting to hear from you now. The rest, of course, is up to you.

If choosing to spend time alone with God is a real struggle—a heavy-handed demand that only adds more guilt and stress to your already overblown schedule—it's time to change the way you approach his presence.

DORIS GREIG

A Gift Beyond Comprehension

Therefore, since we are receiving a kingdom that cannot be shaken, let us hold on to grace. By it, we may serve God acceptably, with reverence and awe.

HEBREWS 12:28 HCSB

The grace of God overflows from His heart. And if we open our hearts to Him, we receive His grace, and we are blessed with joy, abundance, peace, and eternal life.

The familiar words of Ephesians 2:8 make God's promise perfectly clear: "For by grace you have been saved through faith, and that not of yourselves; it is the gift of God" (NKJV). In other words, we are saved, not by our actions, but by God's mercy. We are saved, not because of our good deeds, but because of our faith in Christ.

God's grace is the ultimate gift, a gift beyond comprehension and beyond compare. And because it is the ultimate gift, we owe God the ultimate in thanksgiving.

God's grace is indeed a gift from the heart—God's heart. And as believers, we must accept God's precious gift thankfully, humbly, and, immediately—today is never too soon because tomorrow may be too late.

Our Greatest Refuge

For you have need of endurance, so that when you have done the will of God, you may receive what was promised.

God is our greatest refuge. When every earthly support system fails, God remains steadfast, and His love remains unchanged. When we encounter life's inevitable disappointments and setbacks, God remains faithful. When we suffer loses that leave us breathless, God is always with us, always ready to respond to our prayers, always working in us and through us to turn tragedy into triumph.

Author and speaker Patsy Clairmont observed, "If you are walking toward Jesus to the best of your ability, he will see you through life's unpredictable waters—but you must risk launching the boat." And that's sound advice because even during life's most difficult days, God stands by us. Our job, of course, is to return the favor and stand by Him.

He is within and without. His Spirit dwells within me. His armor protects me. He goes before me and is behind me.

Mary Morrison Suggs

His Healing Touch

"I will give peace, real peace, to those far and near, and I will heal them," says the Lord.

ISAIAH 57:19 NCV

Are you concerned about your spiritual, physical, or emotional health? If so, there is a timeless source of comfort and assurance that is as near as your next breath. That source of comfort, of course, is God.

God is concerned about every aspect of your life, including your health. And, when you face concerns of any sort—including health-related challenges—God is with you. So trust your medical doctor to do his or her part, and turn to your family and friends for moral, physical, and spiritual support. But don't be afraid to place your ultimate trust in your benevolent Heavenly Father. His healing touch, like His love, endures forever.

Jesus Christ is the One by Whom, for Whom, through Whom everything was made. Therefore, He knows what's wrong in your life, and He knows how to fix it.

ANNE GRAHAM LOTZ

God's Gift to You

Everything God made is good, and nothing should be refused if it is accepted with thanks.

1 TIMOTHY 4:4 NCV

Life is God's gift to you, and He intends that you celebrate His glorious gift. If you're a woman who treasures each day, you will be blessed by your Father in heaven.

For Christian believers, every day begins and ends with God and His Son. Christ came to this earth to give us abundant life and eternal salvation. Our task is to accept Christ's grace with joy in our hearts and praise on our lips. Believers who fashion their days around Jesus are transformed: They see the world differently, they act differently, and they feel differently about themselves and their neighbors.

Christian believers face the inevitable challenges and disappointments of each day armed with the joy of Christ and the promise of salvation. So whatever this day holds for you, begin it and end it with God as your partner and Christ as your Savior. And throughout the day, give thanks to the One who created you and saved you. God's love for you is infinite. Accept it joyously and be thankful.

Who Are Our Neighbors?

Never walk away from someone who deserves help; your hand is God's hand for that person.

PROVERBS 3:27 MSG

Who are our neighbors? Jesus answered that question with the story of the Good Samaritan. Our neighbors are any people whom God places in our paths, especially those in need.

We know that we are instructed to love our neighbors, and yet there's so little time...and we're so busy. No matter. As Christians, we are commanded by our Lord and Savior to love our neighbors just as we love ourselves. Period.

This very day, you will encounter someone who needs a word of encouragement, or a pat on the back, or a helping hand, or a heartfelt prayer. And, if you don't reach out to that person, who will? If you don't take the time to understand the needs of your neighbors, who will? If you don't love your brothers and sisters, who will? So, today, look for a neighbor in need...and then do something to help. Father's orders.

The Path He Walked

Therefore as you have received Christ Jesus the Lord, walk in Him.

COLOSSIANS 2:6 HCSB

Today, you will take one more step on your life's journey. Today offers one more opportunity to seek God's will and to follow it. Today has the potential to be a time of praise, a time of thanksgiving, and a time of spiritual abundance. The coming day is a canvas upon which you can compose a beautiful work of art if you choose to do so.

If you choose to follow in the footsteps of the One from Galilee, you will continue to mature every day of your life. If you choose to walk along the path that was first walked by Jesus, your life will become a masterpiece, a powerful work of art, and a tribute to your Savior. So today, as a gift to yourself, to your loved ones, and to your God, walk the path that Jesus walked.

Let us never suppose that obedience is impossible or that holiness is meant only for a select few. Our Shepherd leads us in paths of righteousness—not for our name's sake but for His.

ELISABETH ELLIOT

It Pays to Praise

So through Jesus let us always offer to God our sacrifice of praise, coming from lips that speak his name.

HEBREWS 13:15 NCV

The Bible makes it clear: it pays to praise God. But sometimes, we allow ourselves to become so preoccupied with the demands of everyday life that we forget to say "Thank You" to the Giver of all good gifts.

Worship and praise should be a part of everything we do. Otherwise, we quickly lose perspective as we fall prey to the demands of the moment.

Do you sincerely desire to be a worthy servant of the One who has given you eternal love and eternal life? Then praise Him for who He is and for what He has done for you. And don't just praise Him on Sunday morning. Praise Him all day long, every day, for as long as you live . . . and then for all eternity.

I am to praise God for all things, regardless of where they seem to originate. Doing this is the key to receiving the blessings of God. Praise will wash away my resentments.

CATHERINE MARSHALL

Asking for His Guidance

Ask and it shall be given to you; seek and you shall find; knock and it shall be opened to you. For every one who asks receives, and he who seeks finds, and to him who knocks it shall be opened.

MATTHEW 7:7-8 NASB

Have you fervently asked God for His guidance in every aspect of your life? If so, then you're continually inviting your Creator to reveal Himself in a variety of ways. As a follower of Christ, you must do no less.

Jesus made it clear to His disciples: they should pray always. So should we. Genuine, heartfelt prayer produces powerful changes in us and in our world. When we lift our hearts to our Father in heaven, we open ourselves to a never-ending source of divine wisdom and infinite love.

Do you have questions about your future that you simply can't answer? Ask for the guidance of your heavenly Father. Do you sincerely seek to know God's purpose for your life? Then ask Him for direction—and keep asking Him every day that you live. Whatever your need, no matter how great or small, pray about it and never lose hope. God is not just near; He is here, and He's ready to talk with you. Now!

What to Do?

The lines of purpose in your lives never grow slack, tightly tied as they are to your future in heaven, kept taut by hope.

COLOSSIANS 1:5 MSG

What on earth does God intend for me to do with my life?" It's an easy question to ask but, for many of us, a difficult question to answer. Why? Because God's purposes aren't always clear to us. Sometimes we wander aimlessly in a wilderness of our own making. And sometimes, we struggle mightily against God in an unsuccessful attempt to find success and happiness through our own means, not His.

Sometimes, God's intentions will be clear to you; other times, God's plan will seem uncertain at best. But even on those difficult days when you are unsure which way to turn, you must never lose sight of these overriding facts: God created you for a reason; He has important work for you to do; and He's waiting patiently for you to do it.

And the next step is up to you.

Beyond the Comfort Zone

Be not afraid, only believe.

MARK 5:36 KJV

Risk is an inevitable fact of life. From the moment we arise in the morning until the moment we drift off to sleep at night, we face a wide array of risks, both great and small.

Some risks, of course, should be avoided at all costs—these include risky behaviors that drive us farther and farther away from God's will for our lives. Yet other risks—the kinds of risks that we must take in order to expand our horizons and expand our faith—should be accepted as the inevitable price we must pay for living full and productive lives.

Have you planted yourself firmly inside your own comfort zone? If so, it's time to reconsider the direction and scope of your activities. God has big plans for you, but those plans will most likely require you to expand your comfort zone—or leave it altogether.

Jesus. If you are walking toward him to the best of your ability, he will see you through life's unpredictable waters—but you must risk launching the boat.

PATSY CLAIRMONT

Opportunities for Service

So let us try to do what makes peace and helps one another.

ROMANS 14:19 NCV

You're a special person, created by God, and He has unique work for you to do. Do you acknowledge your own uniqueness, and do you celebrate the one-of-kind opportunities that God has placed before you? Hopefully so. But if you're like too many women, you may have fallen into a trap—the trap of taking yourself and your opportunities for granted.

God created you with a surprising array of talents, and He placed you precisely where you are—at a time and place of His choosing. God has done His part by giving you life, love, blessings, and more opportunities than you can count. Your particular situation is unique and so are your opportunities for service.

And the rest is up to you.

Lovely, complicated wrappings sheath the gift of one-day-more; breathless, I untie the package—never lived this day before!

GLORIA GAITHER

Using Your Talents

God has given gifts to each of you from his great variety of spiritual gifts. Manage them well so that God's generosity can flow through you.

1 PETER 4:10 NLT

Your talents, resources, and opportunities are all gifts from the Giver of all things good. And the best way to say "Thank You" for these gifts is to use them.

Do you have a particular talent? Hone your skill and use it. Do you possess financial resources? Share them. Have you been blessed by a particular opportunity, or have you experienced unusual good fortune? Use your good fortune to help others.

When you share the gifts God has given you—and when you share them freely and without fanfare—you invite God to bless you more and more. So today, do yourself and the world a favor: be a faithful steward of your talents and treasures. And then prepare yourself for even greater blessings that are sure to come.

God has given you special talents—now it's your turn to give them back to God.

MARIE T. FREEMAN

Expecting the Best

Let us hold fast the confession of our hope without wavering, for He who promised is faithful.

HEBREWS 10:23 NKJV

What do you expect from the day ahead? Are you expecting God to do wonderful things, or are you living beneath a cloud of apprehension and doubt? The familiar words of Psalm 118:24 remind us of a profound yet simple truth: God made this day and gave it to us as a gift. We, in response to that gift, should be grateful.

For Christian believers, every day begins and ends with God and His Son. Christ came to this earth to give us abundant life and eternal salvation. We give thanks to our Maker when we treasure each day and use it to the fullest.

Today, let us give thanks for the gift of life and for the One who created it. And then, let's use this day—a precious gift from the Father above—to serve our Savior faithfully, courageously, and joyfully.

Enjoy this day . . . compliments of God.

ANONYMOUS

Seeking His Blessings

Commit everything you do to the Lord. Trust him, and he will help you.

PSALM 37:5 NLT

When our dreams come true and our plans prove successful, we find it easy to thank our Creator and easy to trust His divine providence. But in times of sorrow or hardship, we may find ourselves questioning God's plans for our lives.

On occasion, you will confront circumstances that trouble you to the very core of your soul. It is during these difficult days that you must find the wisdom and the courage to trust your Heavenly Father despite your circumstances.

Are you a woman who seeks God's blessings for yourself and your family? Then trust Him. Trust Him with your relationships. Trust Him with your priorities. Follow His commandments and pray for His guidance. Trust Your Heavenly Father day by day, moment by moment—in good times and in trying times. Then, wait patiently for God's revelations . . . and prepare yourself for the abundance and peace that will most certainly be yours when you do.

God Has Work for You

Work hard, but not just to please your masters when they are watching. As slaves of Christ, do the will of God with all your heart. Work with enthusiasm, as though you were working for the Lord rather than for people.

EPHESIANS 6:6-7 NLT

God has work for you to do, but He won't make you do it. Since the days of Adam and Eve, God has allowed His children to make choices for themselves, and so it is with you. You've got choices to make . . . lots of them. If you choose wisely, you'll be rewarded; if you choose unwisely, you'll bear the consequences.

Whether you're in school or in the workplace, your success will depend, in large part, upon the quality and quantity of your work. God has created a world in which diligence is rewarded and sloth is not. So whatever you choose to do, do it with commitment, excitement, and vigor.

God did not create you for a life of mediocrity; He created you for far greater things. Reaching for greater things usually requires work and lots of it, which is perfectly fine with God. After all, He knows that you're up to the task, and He has big plans for you. Very big plans...

Genuine Peace

These things I have spoken to you, that in Me you may have peace. In the world you will have tribulation; but be of good cheer, I have overcome the world.

JOHN 16:33 NKJV

Have you found the genuine peace that can be yours through Jesus Christ? Or are you still rushing after the illusion of "peace and happiness" that the world promises but cannot deliver? The beautiful words of John 14:27 remind us that Jesus offers us peace, not as the world gives, but as He alone gives. Our challenge is to accept Christ's peace into our hearts and then, as best we can, to share His peace with our neighbors.

Today, as a gift to yourself, to your family, and to your friends, claim the inner peace that is your spiritual birthright: the peace of Jesus Christ. It is offered freely; it has been paid for in full; it is yours for the asking. So ask. And then share.

When we do what is right, we have contentment, peace, and happiness.

BEVERLY LAHAYE

Wisdom and Hope

Know that wisdom is sweet to your soul; if you find it, there is a future hope for you, and your hope will not be cut off.

PROVERBS 24:14 NIV

Wisdom and hope are traveling companions. Wise men and women learn to think optimistically about their lives, their futures, and their faith. The pessimists, however, are not so fortunate; they choose instead to focus their thoughts and energies on faultfinding, criticizing, and complaining, with precious little to show for their efforts.

To become wise, we must seek God's wisdom—the wisdom of hope—and we must live according to God's Word. To become wise, we must seek God's guidance with consistency and purpose. To become wise, we must not only learn the lessons of life, we must live by them.

Do you seek wisdom? Then remember this: The ultimate source of wisdom is the Word of God. When you study God's Word and live according to His commandments, you will grow wise, you will remain hopeful, and you will be a blessing to your family and to the world.

Spiritual Abundance

These things have I spoken unto you, that my joy might remain in you, and that your joy might be full.

John 15:11 KJV

God does not promise us abundance. He promises that we "might have life" and that we "might have it more abundantly" if we accept His grace, His blessings, and His Son (John 10:10). When we commit our hearts and our days to the One who created us, we experience spiritual abundance through the grace and sacrifice of His Son, Jesus. But, when we focus our thoughts and energies, not upon God's perfect will for our lives, but instead upon our own unending assortments of earthly needs and desires, we inevitably forfeit the spiritual abundance that might otherwise be ours.

Today and every day, seek God's will for your life and follow it. Today, turn your worries and your concerns over to your Heavenly Father. Today, seek God's wisdom, follow His commandments, trust His judgment, and honor His Son. When you do, spiritual abundance will be yours, not just for this day, but for all eternity.

The Lessons of Tough Times

No discipline seems pleasant at the time, but painful. Later on, however, it produces a harvest of righteousness and peace for those who have been trained by it.

HEBREWS 12:11 NIV

The times that try your soul are also the times that build your character. During the darker days of life, you can learn lessons that are impossible to learn during sunny, happier days. Times of adversity can—and should—be times of intense spiritual and personal growth. But God will not force you to learn the lessons of adversity. You must learn them for yourself.

The next time Old Man Trouble knocks on your door, remember that he has lessons to teach. So turn away Mr. Trouble as quickly as you can, but as you're doing so, don't forget to learn his lessons. And remember: the trouble with trouble isn't just the trouble it causes; it's also the trouble we cause ourselves if we ignore the things that trouble has to teach. Got that? Then please don't forget it!

It's a good thing to have all the props pulled out from under us occasionally. It gives us some sense of what rock is under our feet, and what is sand. It stops us from taking anything for granted.

MADELEINE L'ENGLE

Obeying God

And we pray this in order that you may live a life worthy of the Lord and may please him in every way: bearing fruit in every good work, growing in the knowledge of God.

COLOSSIANS 1:10 NIV

Each day, we make decisions that can, and should, bring us closer to God. When we live according to God's commandments, we earn for ourselves the abundance and peace that He intends for our lives. But, when we turn our backs upon God by disobeying Him, we bring needless suffering upon ourselves and our families.

Do you seek God's peace and His blessings? Then obey Him. When you're faced with a difficult choice or a powerful temptation, seek God's counsel and trust the counsel He gives. Invite God into your heart and live according to His commandments. When you do, you will be blessed today, and tomorrow, and forever.

Either God's Word keeps you from sin, or sin keeps you from God's Word.

CORRIE TEN BOOM

You can't compromise and conquer sin at the same time.

ANONYMOUS

Celebrating His Gifts

Rejoice, and be exceeding glad: for great is your reward in heaven....

MATTHEW 5:12 KJV

Do you celebrate the gifts God has given you? Do you pray without ceasing? Do you rejoice in the beauty of God's glorious creation? You should. But perhaps, as a busy woman living in a demanding world, you have been slow to count your gifts and even slower to give thanks to the Giver.

As God's children, we are all blessed beyond measure, and we should celebrate His blessings every day that we live. The gifts we receive from God are multiplied when we share them with others. Today is a non-renewable resource—once it's gone, it's gone forever. Our responsibility—as believers—is to give thanks for God's gifts and then use them in the service of God's will and in the service of His people.

God has blessed us beyond measure, and we owe Him everything, including our praise. And let us remember that for those of us who have been saved by God's only begotten Son, every day is a cause for celebration.

When Your Courage Is Tested

But Moses said to the people, "Do not fear! Stand by and see the salvation of the LORD."

EXODUS 14:13 NASB

Jesus has won the victory, so all Christians should live courageously, including you. If you have been touched by the transforming hand of God's Son, then you have every reason to be confident about your future here on earth and your future in heaven. But even if you are a faithful believer, you may find yourself discouraged by the inevitable disappointments and tragedies that are the inevitable price of life here on earth.

If your courage is being tested today, lean upon God's promises. Trust His Son. Remember that God is always near and that He is your protector and your deliverer. When you are worried, anxious, or afraid, call upon Him and accept the touch of His comforting hand. Remember that God rules both mountaintops and valleys—with limitless wisdom and love—now and forever.

As I have grown in faith and confidence, I have known more and more that my worth is based on the love of God.

LESLIE WILLIAMS

Finding Time for God

Every morning he wakes me. He teaches me to listen like a student. The Lord God helps me learn...

ISAIAH 50:4-5 NCV

Each new day is a gift from God, and if we are wise, we spend a few quiet moments each morning thanking the Giver. Daily life is woven together with the threads of habit, and no habit is more important to our spiritual health than the discipline of daily prayer and devotion to the Creator.

When we begin each day with heads bowed and hearts lifted, we remind ourselves of God's love, His protection, and His commandments. And if we are wise, we align our priorities for the coming day with the teachings and commandments that God has given us through His Holy Word.

Are you seeking to change some aspect of your life? Do you seek to improve the condition of your spiritual or physical health? If so, ask for God's help and ask for it many times each day . . . starting with your morning devotional.

I think we Christians have become lazy. We would rather read a book about how someone else became closer to God than spend time alone with him ourselves.

SHEILA WALSH

Encouraging Words for Family and Friends

Do not let any unwholesome talk come out of your mouths, but only what is helpful for building others up according to their needs, that it may benefit those who listen.

EPHESIANS 4:29 NIV

Life is a team sport, and all of us need occasional pats on the back from our teammates. As Christians, we are called upon to spread the Good News of Christ, and we are also called to spread a message of encouragement and hope to the world.

Whether you realize it or not, many people with whom you come in contact every day are in desperate need of a smile or an encouraging word. The world can be a difficult place, and countless friends and family members may be troubled by the challenges of everyday life. Since you don't always know who needs our help, the best strategy is to try to encourage all the people who cross your path. So today, be a world-class source of encouragement to everyone you meet. Never has the need been greater.

True friends will always lift you higher and challenge you to walk in a manner pleasing to our Lord.

LISA BEVERE

Faith and Wholeness

Now the just shall live by faith.

HEBREWS 10:38 NKJV

A suffering woman sought healing in an unusual way: she simply touched the hem of Jesus' garment. When she did, Jesus turned and said, "Daughter, be of good comfort; thy faith hath made thee whole" (Matthew 9:22 KJV). We, too, can be made whole when we place our faith completely and unwaveringly in the person of Jesus Christ.

Concentration camp survivor Corrie ten Boom wrote, "There is no pit so deep that God's love is not deeper still." Christians take note: Genuine faith in God means faith in all circumstances, happy or sad, joyful or tragic.

Your Heavenly Father is standing at the door of your heart. If you reach out to Him in faith, He will give you peace and heal your broken spirit. Be content to touch even the smallest fragment of the Master's garment, and He will make you whole.

Faith is an activity. It is something that has to be applied.

CORRIE TEN BOOM

Your Very Bright Future

For I know the thoughts that I think toward you, says the Lord, thoughts of peace and not of evil, to give you a future and a hope. Then you will call upon Me and go and pray to Me, and I will listen to you.

JEREMIAH 29:11-12 NKJV

How bright is your future? The answer, in all likelihood, is that your future is so bright that you'd better wear shades!

Now, here's something else to ponder: How bright do you believe your future to be? Are you expecting a terrific tomorrow, or are you dreading a terrible one? And make no mistake: the answer to this second set of questions will have a powerful impact on the way tomorrow turns out.

Corrie ten Boom had this advice: "Never be afraid to trust an unknown future to a known God." And it's advice that most certainly applies to you. So, with no further ado, it's time to trust God . . . and put on the shades.

Yesterday is just experience but tomorrow is glistening with purpose—and today is the channel leading from one to the other.

BARBARA JOHNSON

Heeding His Call

I, therefore, the prisoner in the Lord, urge you to walk worthy of the calling you have received.

EPHESIANS 4:1 HCSB

It is terribly important that you heed God's calling by discovering and developing your talents and your spiritual gifts. If you seek to make a difference—and if you seek to bear eternal fruit—you must discover your gifts and begin using them for the glory of God.

Every believer has at least one gift. In John 15:16, Jesus says, "You did not choose Me, but I chose you and appointed you that you should go and bear fruit, and that your fruit should remain, that whatever you ask the Father in My name He may give you." Have you found your special calling? If not, keep searching and keep praying until you find it. God has important work for you to do, and the time to begin that work is now.

If God has called you, do not spend time looking over your shoulder to see who is following you.

CORRIE TEN BOOM

Limitless Power, Limitless Love

Enter his gates with thanksgiving; go into his courts with praise. Give thanks to him and bless his name. For the Lord is good. His unfailing love continues forever, and his faithfulness continues to each generation.

PSALM 100:4-5 NLT

Because God's power is limitless, it is far beyond the comprehension of mortal minds. But even though we cannot fully understand the heart of God, we can be open to God's love.

God's ability to love is not burdened by temporal boundaries or by earthly limitations. The love that flows from the heart of God is infinite—and today presents yet another opportunity to celebrate that love.

You are a glorious creation, a unique individual, a beautiful example of God's handiwork. God's love for you is limitless. Accept that love, acknowledge it, and be grateful.

Everything I possess of any worth is a direct product of God's love.

BETH MOORE

God's Sufficiency

My grace is sufficient for you, for My strength is made perfect in weakness.

2 CORINTHIANS 12:9 NKJV

O f this you can be sure: the loving heart of God is sufficient to meet your needs. Whatever dangers you may face, whatever heartbreaks you must endure, God is with you, and He stands ready to comfort you and to heal you.

The Psalmist writes, "Weeping may endure for a night, but joy comes in the morning" (Psalm 30:5 NKJV). But when we are suffering, the morning may seem very far away. It is not. God promises that He is "near to those who have a broken heart" (Psalm 34:18 NKJV). In times of intense sadness, we must turn to Him, and we must encourage our friends and family members to do likewise.

If you are experiencing the intense pain of a recent loss, or if you are still mourning a loss from long ago, perhaps you are now ready to begin the next stage of your journey with God. If so, be mindful of this fact: the loving heart of God is sufficient to meet any challenge, including yours. Trust the sufficient heart of God.

Guard Your Heart

Guard your heart above all else, for it is the source of life.
PROVERBS 4:23 HCSB

You are near and dear to God. He loves you more than you can imagine, and He wants the very best for you. And one more thing: God wants you to guard your heart.

Every day, you are faced with choices . . . lots of them. You can do the right thing, or not. You can tell the truth, or not. You can be kind, and generous, and obedient. Or not.

Your mind and your heart will usually tell you the right thing to do. And if you listen to your friends and family, they will help you, too, by teaching you God's rules. Then, you will learn that doing the right thing is always better than doing the wrong thing. And, by obeying God's rules, you will guard your heart by giving it to His Son Jesus.

The fruit of our placing all things in God's hands is the presence of His abiding peace in our hearts.
HANNAH WHITALL SMITH

Sharing the Joy

Let the hearts of those who seek the Lord rejoice. Look to the Lord and his strength; seek his face always.

1 CHRONICLES 16:10-11 NIV

God intends that His joy should become our joy. He intends that we, His children, should share His love, His joy, and His peace. Yet sometimes, amid the rush of our daily lives, we don't feel much like sharing. So we forfeit—albeit temporarily—God's joy as we wrestle with the challenges of everyday life.

If, today, your heart is heavy, open the door of your soul to your Heavenly Father. When you do, He will renew your spirit. And, if you already have the joy of Christ in your heart, share it freely. When you discover ways to make your joy become their joy, you will have discovered a wonderful way to say, "I love you" to your family, to your friends, and, most especially, to your God.

According to Jesus, it is God's will that His children be filled with the joy of life.

CATHERINE MARSHALL

Swamped by Your Possessions?

Don't be obsessed with getting more material things. Be relaxed with what you have.

HEBREWS 13:5 MSG

Do you sometimes feel swamped by your possessions? Do you seem to spending more and more time keep track of the things you own while making mental notes of the things you intend to buy? If so, here's a word of warning: your fondness for material possessions is getting in the way of your relationships— your relationships with the people around you and your relationship with God.

Society teaches us to honor possessions . . . God teaches us to honor people. And if we seek to be worthy followers of Christ, we must never invest too much energy in the acquisition of "stuff." Earthly riches are here today and all too soon gone. Our real riches, of course, are in heaven, and that's where we should focus our thoughts and our energy.

It's sobering to contemplate how much time, effort, sacrifice, compromise, and attention we give to acquiring and increasing our supply of something that is totally insignificant in eternity.

ANNE GRAHAM LOTZ

A Heart Aflame?

Whatever work you do, do your best, because you are going to the grave, where there is no working . . . .
ECCLESIASTES 9:10 NCV

We have every reason to be enthusiastic about life, but sometimes the struggles of daily living may cause us to feel decidedly unenthusiastic. Whenever we feel our energies begin to fade, it's time to slow down, to rest, to count our blessings, and to have a sensible talk with God. When we feel worried or weary, a few moments spent in quiet conversation with the Creator can calm our fears and restore our perspective.

Mary Lou Retton observed, "Heat is required to forge anything. Every great accomplishment is the story of a flaming heart." Is your heart aflame? Are you fully engaged in life—and in love? If so, keep up the good work! But if you feel the passion slowly draining from your life, it's time to refocus your thoughts, your energies, and your prayers . . . now.

Give me the love that leads the way, the faith that nothing can dismay, the hope no disappointments tire, the passion that will burn like fire. Let me not sink to be a clod: Make me thy fuel, flame of God.

AMY CARMICHAEL

A Marathon

Therefore since we also have such a large cloud of witnesses surrounding us, let us lay aside every weight and the sin that so easily ensnares us, and run with endurance the race that lies before us.

HEBREWS 12:1 HCSB

A well-lived life is like a marathon, not a sprint—it calls for preparation, determination, and lots of perseverance. As an example of perfect perseverance, we Christians need look no further than our Savior, Jesus Christ.

Jesus finished what He began. Despite His suffering, despite the shame of the cross, Jesus was steadfast in His faithfulness to God. We, too, must remain faithful, especially during times of hardship. Sometimes, God may answer our prayers with silence, and when He does, we must patiently persevere.

Are you facing a difficult time in your life? If so, remember the words of Winston Churchill: "Never give in!" And remember this: whatever your problem, God can handle it. Your job is to keep persevering until He does.

Your Primary Obligation

Everything that goes into a life of pleasing God has been miraculously given to us by getting to know, personally and intimately, the One who invited us to God. The best invitation we ever received!

2 PETER 1:3 MSG

When God created you, he equipped you with an assortment of talents and abilities that are uniquely yours. It's up to you to discover those talents and to use them, but the world may encourage you to do otherwise. At times, society will attempt to pigeonhole you, to standardize you, and to make you fit into a particular, preformed mold. Perhaps God has other plans.

At times, because you're an imperfect human being, you may become so wrapped up in meeting society's expectations that you fail to focus on God's expectations.

Who will you try to please today: God or society? Your primary obligation is not to please imperfect men and women. Your obligation is to strive diligently to meet the expectations of an all-knowing and perfect God. Period.

Pray Always

Watch therefore, and pray always that you may be counted worthy . . . .

LUKE 21:36 NKJV

Jesus made it clear to His disciples: they should pray always. And so should we. Genuine, heartfelt prayer changes things and it changes us. When we lift our hearts to our Father in heaven, we open ourselves to a never-ending source of divine wisdom and infinite love.

Do you have questions that you simply can't answer? Ask for the guidance of your Father in heaven. Do you sincerely seek the gift of everlasting love and eternal life? Accept the grace of God's only begotten Son. Whatever your need, no matter how great or small, pray about it. Instead of waiting for mealtimes or bedtimes, follow the instruction of your Savior: pray always and never lose heart. And remember: God is not just near; He is here, and He's ready to talk with you. Now!

Prayer moves the arm that moves the world.

ANNIE ARMSTRONG

Jesus practiced secret prayer and asked us to follow His example.

CATHERINE MARSHALL

What Now, Lord?

For we are His making, created in Christ Jesus for good works, which God prepared ahead of time so that we should walk in them.

EPHESIANS 2:10 HCSB

God has things He wants you to do and places He wants you to go. The most important decision of your life is, of course, your commitment to accept Jesus Christ as your personal Lord and Savior. And, once your eternal destiny is secured, you will undoubtedly ask yourself the question "What now, Lord?" If you earnestly seek God's will for your life, you will find it . . . in time.

As you prayerfully consider God's path for your life, you should study His Word and be ever watchful for His signs. You should associate with fellow believers who will encourage your spiritual growth, and you should listen to that inner voice of your conscience.

As you continually seek God's purpose for your life, be patient: your Heavenly Father may not always reveal himself as quickly as you would like. But rest assured: God is here, and He intends to use you in wonderful, unexpected ways. Your challenge is to watch, to listen . . . and to follow.

Real Repentance

Come back to the LORD and live!

AMOS 5:6 NLT

Genuine repentance requires more than simply offering God apologies for our misdeeds. Real repentance may start with feelings of sorrow and remorse, but it ends only when we turn away from the sin that has heretofore distanced us from our Creator. In truth, we offer our most meaningful apologies to God, not with our words, but with our actions. As long as we are still engaged in sin, we may be "repenting," but we have not fully "repented."

Is there an aspect of your life that is distancing you from your God? If so, ask for His forgiveness, and—just as importantly—stop sinning. Then, wrap yourself in the protection of God's Word. When you do, you will be secure.

God's presence is such a cleansing fire, confession and repentance are always there.

ANNE ORTLUND

The Heart of a Servant

The one who blesses others is abundantly blessed; those who help others are helped.

PROVERBS 11:25 MSG

You are a wondrous creation treasured by God . . . how will you respond? Will you consider each day a glorious opportunity to celebrate life and improve your little corner of the world? Hopefully so because your corner of the world, like so many other corners of the world, can use all the help it can get.

Nicole Johnson observed, "We only live once, and if we do it well, once is enough." Her words apply to you. You can make a difference, a big difference in the quality of your own life and lives of your neighbors, your family, and your friends.

You make the world a better place whenever you find a need and fill it. And in these difficult days, the needs are great—but so are your abilities to meet those needs.

We can love Jesus in the hungry, the naked, and the destitute who are dying...If you love, you will be willing to serve. And you will find Jesus in the distressing disguise of the poor.

MOTHER TERESA

Searching for Strength

God is our refuge and strength, a very present help in trouble.

PSALM 46:1 NKJV

Where do you go to find strength? The gym? The health food store? The espresso bar? There's a better source of strength, of course, and that source is God. He is a never-ending source of strength and courage if you call upon Him.

Are you an energized Christian? You should be. But if you're not, you must seek strength and renewal from the source that will never fail: that source, of course, is your Heavenly Father. And rest assured—when you sincerely petition Him, He will give you all the strength you need to live victoriously for Him.

Have you "tapped in" to the power of God? Have you turned your life and your heart over to Him, or are you muddling along under your own power? The answer to this question will determine the quality of your life here on earth and the destiny of your life throughout all eternity. So start tapping in—and remember that when it comes to strength, God is the Ultimate Source.

Focusing on Your Hopes

This hope we have as an anchor of the soul, both sure and steadfast, and which enters the Presence behind the veil.
HEBREWS 6:19 NKJV

Paul Valéry observed, "We hope vaguely but dread precisely." How true. All too often, we allow the worries of everyday life to overwhelm our thoughts and cloud our vision. What's needed is clearer perspective, renewed faith, and a different focus.

When we focus on the frustrations of today or the uncertainties of tomorrow, we rob ourselves of peace in the present moment. But, when we focus on God's grace, and when we trust in the ultimate wisdom of God's plan for our lives, our worries no longer tyrannize us.

Today, remember that God is infinitely greater than the challenges that you face. Remember also that your thoughts are profoundly powerful, so guard them accordingly.

As we have by faith said no to sin, so we should by faith say yes to God and set our minds on things above, where Christ is seated in the heavenlies.

VONETTE BRIGHT

Actions Speak Louder

Are there those among you who are truly wise and understanding? Then they should show it by living right and doing good things with a gentleness that comes from wisdom.

JAMES 3:13 NCV

The old saying is both familiar and true: actions speak louder than words. And as believers, we must beware: our actions should always give credence to the changes that Christ can make in the lives of those who walk with Him.

God calls upon each of us to act in accordance with His will and with respect for His commandments. If we are to be responsible believers, we must realize that it is never enough simply to hear the instructions of God; we must also live by them. And it is never enough to wait idly by while others do God's work here on earth; we, too, must act. Doing God's work is a responsibility that each of us must bear, and when we do, our loving Heavenly Father rewards our efforts with a bountiful harvest.

God has lots of folks who intend to go to work for him "some day." What He needs is more people who are willing to work for Him this day.

MARIE T. FREEMAN

Restoring Your Hope

Until now you have not asked for anything in my name. Ask and you will receive, so that your joy will be the fullest possible joy.

JOHN 16:24 NCV

Have you fervently asked God to restore your hope for tomorrow? Have you asked Him for guidance and strength? If so, then you're continually inviting your Creator to reveal Himself in a variety of ways. As a follower of Christ, you must do no less.

Jesus made it clear to His disciples: they should petition God to meet their needs. So should we. Genuine, heartfelt prayer produces powerful changes in us and in our world. When we lift our hearts to God, we open ourselves to a never-ending source of divine wisdom and infinite love.

Do you have questions about your future that you simply can't answer? Do you have needs that you simply can't meet by yourself? Do you sincerely seek to know God's purpose for your life? If so, ask Him for direction, for protection, and for strength—and then keep asking Him every day. Whatever your need, no matter how great or small, pray about it and never lose hope. God is not just near; He is here, and He's perfectly capable of answering your prayers. Now, it's up to you to ask.

Sharing Your Burdens

The LORD himself goes before you and will be with you; he will never leave you nor forsake you. Do not be afraid; do not be discouraged.

DEUTERONOMY 31:8 NIV

The Bible promises this: tough times are temporary but God's love is not—God's love endures forever. So what does that mean to you? Just this: From time to time, everybody faces hardships and disappointments, and so will you. And when tough times arrive, God always stands ready to protect you and to heal you. Your task is straightforward: you must share your burdens with Him.

Whatever the size of your challenges, God is big enough to handle them. Ask for His help today, with faith and with fervor. Instead of turning things over in your mind, turn them over to God in prayer. Instead of worrying about your next decision, ask God to lead the way. Cast your burdens upon the One who cannot be shaken, and rest assured that He always hears your prayers.

Real Christianity

But now in Christ Jesus you who formerly were far off have been brought near by the blood of Christ. For He Himself is our peace.

EPHESIANS 2:13-14 NASB

What is "real" Christianity? Think of it as an ongoing relationship—an all-encompassing relationship with God and with His Son Jesus. It is inevitable that your life must be lived in relationship to God. The question is not if you will have a relationship with Him; the burning question is whether or not that relationship will be one that seeks to honor Him or one that seeks to ignore Him.

We live in a world that discourages heartfelt devotion and obedience to God. Everywhere we turn, or so it seems, we are confronted by a mind-numbing assortment of distractions, temptations, obligations, and frustrations. Yet even on our busiest days, God beckons us to slow down and consult Him. When we do, we avail ourselves of the peace and abundance that only He can give.

The empty tomb proves Christianity. The empty church denies it.

ANONYMOUS

Courtesy Matters

Be hospitable to one another without grumbling.

1 PETER 4:9 NKJV

Did Christ instruct us in matters of etiquette and courtesy? Of course He did. Christ's instructions are clear: "In everything, therefore, treat people the same way you want them to treat you, for this is the Law and the Prophets" (Matthew 7:12 NASB). Jesus did not say, "In some things, treat people as you wish to be treated." And, He did not say, "From time to time, treat others with kindness." Christ said that we should treat others as we wish to be treated in every aspect of our daily lives. This, of course, is a tall order indeed, but as Christians, we are commanded to do our best.

Today, be a little kinder than necessary to family members, friends, and total strangers. And, as you consider all the things that Christ has done in your life, honor Him with your words and with your deeds. He expects no less, and He deserves no less.

Reach out and care for someone who needs the touch of hospitality. The time you spend caring today will be a love gift that will blossom into the fresh joy of God's Spirit in the future.

EMILIE BARNES

Beyond Doubt

Now if any of you lacks wisdom, he should ask God, who gives to all generously and without criticizing, and it will be given to him. But let him ask in faith without doubting. For the doubter is like the surging sea, driven and tossed by the wind.

JAMES 1:5-6 HCSB

If you've never had any doubts about your faith, then you can stop reading this page now and skip to the next. But if you've ever been plagued by doubts about your faith or your God, keep reading.

Even some of the most faithful Christians are, at times, beset by occasional bouts of discouragement and doubt. But even when we feel far removed from God, God is never far removed from us. He is always with us, always willing to calm the storms of life—always willing to replace our doubts with comfort and assurance.

Whenever you're plagued by doubts, that's precisely the moment you should seek God's presence by genuinely seeking to establish a deeper, more meaningful relationship with His Son. Then you may rest assured that in time, God will calm your fears, answer your prayers, and restore your confidence.

Eternal Life: God's Priceless Gift

Jesus said, "Everyone who drinks from this water will get thirsty again. But whoever drinks from the water that I will give him will never get thirsty again--ever! In fact, the water I will give him will become a well of water springing up within him for eternal life."

JOHN 4:13-14 HCSB

Your ability to envision the future, like your life here on earth, is limited. God's vision, however, is not burdened by any such limitations. He sees all things, He knows all things, and His plans for you endure for all time.

God's plans are not limited to the events of life-here-on-earth. Your Heavenly Father has bigger things in mind for you . . . much bigger things. So praise the Creator for the gift of eternal life and share the Good News with all who cross your path. You have given your heart to the Son, so you belong to the Father—today, tomorrow, and for all eternity.

Your choice to either receive or reject the Lord Jesus Christ will determine where you spend eternity.

ANNE GRAHAM LOTZ

Follow Him

If anyone serves Me, let him follow Me; and where I am, there My servant will be also. If anyone serves Me, him My Father will honor.

JOHN 12:26 NKJV

Jesus walks with you. Are you walking with Him? Hopefully, you will choose to walk with Him today and every day of your life.

Jesus loved you so much that He endured unspeakable humiliation and suffering for you. How will you respond to Christ's sacrifice? Will you take up His cross and follow Him (Luke 9:23) or will you choose another path? When you place your hopes squarely at the foot of the cross, when you place Jesus squarely at the center of your life, you will be blessed. If you seek to be a worthy disciple of Jesus, you must acknowledge that He never comes "next." He is always first.

Do you hope to fulfill God's purpose for your life? Do you seek a life of abundance and peace? Do you intend to be Christian, not just in name, but in deed? Then follow Christ. Follow Him by picking up His cross today and every day that you live. When you do, you will quickly discover that Christ's love has the power to change everything, including you.

Who Rules?

You shall have no other gods before Me.

EXODUS 20:3 NKJV

Who rules your heart? Is it God, or is it something else? Do you give God your firstfruits or your last? Have you given Christ your heart, your soul, your talents, your time, and your testimony, or have you given Him little more than a few hours each Sunday morning?

In the book of Exodus, God warns that we should place no gods before Him. Yet all too often, we place our Lord in second, third, or fourth place as we worship the gods of pride, greed, power, or lust. When we unwittingly place possessions or relationships above our love for the Creator, we must seek His forgiveness and repent from our sins.

Does God rule your heart? Make certain that the honest answer to this question is a resounding yes. In the life of every righteous believer, God comes first. And that's precisely the place that He deserves in your heart.

God is everything. My focus must be on him, seeking to know him more completely and allowing him full possession of my life.

MARY MORRISON SUGGS

How Much Does God Love You?

For God loved the world in this way: He gave His only Son, so that everyone who believes in Him will not perish but have eternal life.

JOHN 3:16 HCSB

How much does God love you? To answer that question, you need only to look at the cross. God's love for you is so great that He sent His only Son to this earth to die for your sins and to offer you the priceless gift of eternal life.

You must decide whether or not to accept God's gift. Will you ignore it or embrace it? Will you return it or neglect it? Will you invite Christ to dwell in the center of your heart, or will you relegate Him to a position of lesser importance? The decision is yours, and so are the consequences. So choose wisely . . . and choose today.

There is no creature made who can realize how much, how sweetly, and how tenderly our Maker loves us. And therefore we can, with His grace and His help, stand in spirit, gazing with endless wonder at this lofty, immeasurable love—beyond human scope—that the Almighty, in His goodness, has for us.

JULIANA OF NORWICH

He Cares for You

And God will generously provide all you need. Then you will always have everything you need and plenty left over to share with others.

2 CORINTHIANS 9:8 NLT

The Bible makes this promise: God will care for you and protect you. In the 6th Chapter of Matthew, Jesus made this point clear when He said,

Do not worry about your life, what you will eat or what you will drink; nor about your body, what you will put on. Is not life more than food and the body more than clothing? Look at the birds of the air, for they neither sow nor reap nor gather into barns; yet your heavenly Father feeds them. Are you not of more value than they? Which of you by worrying can add one cubit to his stature? . . . Therefore do not worry about tomorrow, for tomorrow will worry about its own things. Sufficient for the day is its own trouble (25-27, 34 NKJV).

This beautiful passage reminds you that God still sits in His heaven and you are His beloved child. Simply put, you are protected.

I am grateful that when even a single sparrow falls to the ground, God knows—and understands.

RUTH BELL GRAHAM

Filled by the Spirit

I will put my Spirit in you and you will live....

EZEKIEL 37:14 NIV

Are you burdened by the pressures of everyday living? If so, it's time to take the pressure off. How can you do so? By allowing the Holy Spirit to fill you and do His work in your life.

When you are filled with the Holy Spirit, your words and deeds will reflect a love and devotion to Christ. When you are filled with the Holy Spirit, the steps of your life's journey are guided by the Lord. When you allow God's Spirit to work in you and through you, you will be energized and transformed.

Today, allow yourself to be filled with the Spirit of God. And then stand back in amazement as God begins to work miracles in your own life and in the lives of those you love.

The Holy Spirit will not come to us in his fullness until we see and assent to his priority—his passion for ministry.

CATHERINE MARSHALL

The Glorious Gift of Life

Seek the Lord, and ye shall live....

AMOS 5:6 KJV

L ife is a glorious gift from God. Treat it that way.

This day, like every other, is filled to the brim with opportunities, challenges, and choices. But, no choice that you make is more important than the choice you make concerning God. Today, you will either place Him at the center of your life—or not—and the consequences of that choice have implications that are both temporal and eternal.

Sometimes, we don't intentionally neglect God; we simply allow ourselves to become overwhelmed with the demands of everyday life. And then, without our even realizing it, we gradually drift away from the One we need most. Thankfully, God never drifts away from us. He remains always present, always steadfast, always loving.

As you begin this day, place God and His Son where they belong: in your head, in your prayers, on your lips, and in your heart. And then, with God as your guide and companion, let the journey begin . . .

Faith-filled Christianity

Commit your works to the Lord, and your thoughts will be established.

As you take the next step in your life's journey, you should do so with feelings of hope and anticipation. After all, as a Christian, you have every reason to be optimistic about life. As John Calvin observed, "There is not one blade of grass, there is no color in this world that is not intended to make us rejoice." But, sometimes, rejoicing may be the last thing on your mind. Sometimes, you may fall prey to worry, frustration, anxiety, or sheer exhaustion. What's needed is plenty of rest, a large dose of perspective, and God's healing touch, but not necessarily in that order.

A. W. Tozer writes, "Attitude is all-important. Let the soul take a quiet attitude of faith and love toward God, and from there on, the responsibility is God's. He will make good on His commitments." These words remind us that even when the challenges of the day seem daunting, God remains steadfast. And, so must we.

His Path

The LORD says, "I will guide you along the best pathway for your life. I will advise you and watch over you."

PSALM 32:8 NLT

How will you respond to Christ's sacrifice? Will you take up His cross and follow Him (Luke 9:23) or will you choose another path? When you place your hopes squarely at the foot of the cross, when you place Jesus squarely at the center of your life, you will be blessed.

The 19th-century writer Hannah Whitall Smith observed, "The crucial question for each of us is this: What do you think of Jesus, and do you yet have a personal acquaintance with Him?" Indeed, the answer to that question determines the quality, the course, and the direction of our lives today and for all eternity.

Let us put down our old ways and pick us His cross. Let us walk the path that He walked.

We are meddling with God's business when we let all manner of imaginings loose, predicting disaster, contemplating possibilities instead of following, one day at a time, God's plain and simple pathway.

ELISABETH ELLIOT

Peace and Prayer

Be cheerful no matter what; pray all the time; thank God no matter what happens. This is the way God wants you who belong to Christ Jesus to live.

1 Thessalonians 5:16-18 MSG

Do you seek a more peaceful life? Then you must lead a prayerful life. Do you have questions that you simply can't answer? Ask for the guidance of your Father in heaven. Do you sincerely seek the gift of everlasting love and eternal life? Accept the grace of God's only begotten Son.

When you weave the habit of prayer into the very fabric of your day, you invite God to become a partner in every aspect of your life. When you consult God on an constant basis, you avail yourself of His wisdom, His strength, and His love. And, because God answers prayers according to His perfect timetable, your petitions to Him will transform your family, your world, and yourself.

Today, turn everything over to your Creator in prayer. Instead of worrying about your next decision, decide to let God lead the way. Don't limit your prayers to meals or to bedtime. Pray constantly about things great and small. God is listening, and He wants to hear from you. Now.

Trusting His Answers

*Trust in the LORD with all your heart; do not depend on
your own understanding.*

PROVERBS 3:5 NLT

God answers our prayers. What God does not do
is this: He does not always answer our prayers as
soon as we might like, and He does not always answer
our prayers by saying "Yes." God isn't an order-taker,
and He's not some sort of cosmic vending machine.
Sometimes—even when we want something very
badly—our loving Heavenly Father responds to our
requests by saying "No", and we must accept His answer,
even if we don't understand it.

God answers prayers not only according to our
wishes but also according to His master plan. We
cannot know that plan, but we can know the Planner . . .
and we must trust His wisdom, His righteousness, and
His love. Always.

Often I have made a request of God with earnest
pleadings even backed up with Scripture, only to have
Him say "No" because He had something better in
store.

RUTH BELL GRAHAM

Renewal and Celebration

And He who sits on the throne said, "Behold, I am making all things new."

REVELATION 21:5 NASB

Each new day offers countless opportunities to celebrate life and to serve God's children. But each day also offers countless opportunities to fall prey to the countless distractions of our difficult age.

Consider this day a new beginning. Consider it a fresh start, a renewed opportunity to serve your friends and family with willing hands and a loving heart.

Gigi Graham Tchividjian spoke for women everywhere when she observed, "How much of our lives are, well, so daily. How often our hours are filled with the mundane, seemingly unimportant things that have to be done, whether at home or work. These very 'daily' tasks could—and should—become a celebration."

Make your life a celebration. After all, your talents are unique, as are your opportunities. So the best time to really live—and really celebrate—is now.

He is the God of wholeness and restoration.

STORMIE OMARTIAN

His Plan for You

For I am not ashamed of this Good News about Christ. It is the power of God at work, saving everyone who believes.

ROMANS 1:16 NLT

How marvelous it is that God became a man and walked among us. Had He not chosen to do so, we might feel removed from a distant Creator. But ours is not a distant God. Ours is a God who understands—far better than we ever could—the essence of what it means to be human.

God understands our hopes, our fears, and our temptations. He understands what it means to be angry and what it costs to forgive. He knows the heart, the conscience, and the soul of every person who has ever lived, including you. And God has a plan of salvation that is intended for you. Accept it. Accept God's gift through the person of His Son Christ Jesus, and then rest assured: God walked among us so that you might have eternal life; amazing though it may seem, He did it for you.

Just as I am, without one plea, but that Thy blood was shed for me. And that Thou bid'st me come to Thee, O Lamb of God, I come! I come!

CHARLOTTE ELLIOTT

Helpful Words

Careful words make for a careful life; careless talk may ruin everything.

PROVERBS 13:3 MSG

This world can be a difficult place, a place where many of our friends and family members are troubled by the inevitable challenges of everyday life. And since we can never be certain who needs our help, we should be careful to speak helpful words to everybody who crosses our paths.

In the book of Ephesians, Paul writes, "Do not let any unwholesome talk come out of your mouths, but only what is helpful for building others up according to their needs, that it may benefit those who listen" (4:29 NIV). Paul reminds us that when we choose our words carefully, we can have a powerful impact on those around us.

Today, let's share kind words, smiles, encouragement, and hugs with family, with friends, and with the world.

When you talk, choose the very same words that you would use if Jesus were looking over your shoulder. Because He is.

MARIE T. FREEMAN

What We Become

For it is God who is working among you both the willing and the working for His good purpose.

PHILIPPIANS 2:13 HCSB

The old saying is both familiar and true: "What we are is God's gift to us; what we become is our gift to God." Each of us possesses special talents, gifted by God, that can be nurtured carefully or ignored totally. Our challenge, of course, is to use our abilities to the greatest extent possible and to use them in ways that honor our Savior.

Are you using your natural talents to make God's world a better place? If so, congratulations. But if you have gifts that you have not fully explored and developed, perhaps you need to have a chat with the One who gave you those gifts in the first place. Your talents are priceless treasures offered from your Heavenly Father. Use them. After all, an obvious way to say "thank you" to the Giver is to use the gifts He has given.

Faith Tip:
Today, take time to think about ways you can convert talent into results.

This Is the Day

This is the day the LORD has made; let us rejoice and be glad in it.

PSALM 118:24 NIV

The familiar words of Psalm 118:24 remind us of a profound yet simple truth: God created this day, and it's up to each of us to rejoice and to be grateful.

For Christian believers, every day begins and ends with God and His Son. Christ came to this earth to give us abundant life and eternal salvation. We give thanks to our Maker when we treasure each day and use it to the fullest.

This day is a gift from God. How will you use it? Will you celebrate God's gifts and obey His commandments? Will you share words of encouragement and hope with all who cross your path? Will you share the Good News of the risen Christ? Will you trust in the Father and praise His glorious handiwork? The answer to these questions will determine, to a surprising extent, the direction and the quality of your day.

So whatever this day holds for you, begin it and end it with God as your partner and Christ as your Savior. And throughout the day, give thanks to the One who created you and saved you. God's love for you is infinite. Accept it joyously and be thankful.

Bearing Witness to the Truth

But the natural man does not welcome what comes from God's Spirit, because it is foolishness to him; he is not able to know it since it is evaluated spiritually. The spiritual person, however, can evaluate everything, yet he himself cannot be evaluated by anyone.

1 CORINTHIANS 2:14-15 HCSB

When God's spirit touches our hearts, we are confronted by a powerful force: the awesome, irresistible force of God's Truth. In response to that force, we will either follow God's lead by allowing Him to guide our thoughts and deeds, or we will resist God's calling and accept the consequences of our rebellion.

Today, as you fulfill the responsibilities that God has placed before you, ask yourself this question: "Do my thoughts and actions bear witness to the ultimate Truth that God has placed in my heart, or am I allowing the pressures of everyday life to overwhelm me?" It's a profound question that only you can answer. You be the judge.

When you don't witness, you just did.

ANONYMOUS

The Treasure Hunt

For where your treasure is, there will your heart be also.
LUKE 12:34 KJV

All of mankind is engaged in a colossal, worldwide treasure hunt. Some people seek treasure from earthly sources, treasures such as material wealth or public acclaim; others seek God's treasures by making Him the cornerstone of their lives.

What kind of treasure hunter are you? Are you so caught up in the demands of everyday living that you sometimes allow the search for worldly treasures to become your primary focus? If so, it's time to reorganize your daily to-do list by placing God in His rightful place: first place. Don't allow anyone or anything to separate you from your Heavenly Father and His only begotten Son.

The world's treasures are difficult to find and difficult to keep; God's treasures are ever-present and everlasting. Which treasures, then, will you claim as your own?

I have a divided heart, trying to love God and the world at the same time. God says, "You can't love me as you should if you love this world too."

MARY MORRISON SUGGS

Peace and His Word

Great peace have they which love thy law.

PSALM 119:165 KJV

Do you seek God's peace? Then study His Word. God's Word is unlike any other book. The Bible is a roadmap for life here on earth and for life eternal. As Christians, we are called upon to study God's Holy Word, to trust His Word, to follow its commandments, and to share its Good News with the world.

The words of Matthew 4:4 remind us that, "Man shall not live by bread alone but by every word that proceedeth out of the mouth of God" (KJV). As believers, we must study the Bible and meditate upon its meaning for our lives. Otherwise, we deprive ourselves of a priceless gift from our Creator.

A passing acquaintance with the Good Book is insufficient for Christians who seek to obey God's Word and to understand His will. After all, man does not live by bread alone . . .

God has revealed to us a new reality that the world does not understand: In his eternal kingdom, what matters is being like our Father. That is the way to success and peace.

MARY MORRISON SUGGS

When We Lose Hope

Be of good courage, and He shall strengthen your heart, all you who hope in the Lord.

PSALM 31:24 NKJV

As every woman knows, hope is a perishable commodity. Despite God's promises, despite Christ's love, and despite our countless blessings, we frail human beings can still lose hope from time to time. When we do, we need the encouragement of Christian friends, the life-changing power of prayer, and the healing truth of God's Holy Word. If we find ourselves falling into the spiritual traps of worry and discouragement, we should seek the healing touch of Jesus and the encouraging words of fellow Christians. Even though this world can be a place of trials and struggles, God has promised us peace, joy, and eternal life if we give ourselves to Him.

Are you a Christian? If you are, how can you be hopeless? Are you so depressed by the greatness of your problems that you have given up all hope? Instead of giving up, would you patiently endure? Would you focus on Christ until you are so preoccupied with him alone that you fall prostrate before him?

ANNE GRAHAM LOTZ

The Abundant Life

A thief comes to steal and kill and destroy, but I came to give life—life in all its fullness.

JOHN 10:10 NCV

When Jesus talks of the abundant life, is he talking about material riches or earthly fame? Hardly. The Son of God came to this world, not to give it prosperity, but to give it salvation. Thankfully for Christians, our Savior's abundance is both spiritual and eternal; it never falters—even if we do—and it never dies. We need only to open our hearts to Him, and His grace becomes ours.

God's gifts are available to all, but they are not guaranteed; those gifts must be claimed by those who choose to follow Christ. As believers, we are free to accept God's gifts, or not; that choice, and the consequences that result from it, are ours and ours alone.

As we go about our daily lives, may we accept God's promise of spiritual abundance, and may we share it with a world in desperate need of the Master's healing touch.

It would be wrong to have a "poverty complex," for to think ourselves paupers is to deny either the King's riches or to deny our being His children.

CATHERINE MARSHALL

The Tapestry of Life

Let not your heart be troubled; you believe in God, believe also in Me. In My Father's house are many mansions; if it were not so, I would have told you. I go to prepare a place for you. And if I go and prepare a place for you, I will come again and receive you to Myself; that where I am, there you may be also.

JOHN 14:1-3 NKJV

Life is a tapestry of good days and difficult days, with good days predominating. During the good days, we are tempted to take our blessings for granted (a temptation that we must resist with all our might). But, during life's difficult days, we discover precisely what we're made of. And more importantly, we discover what our faith is made of.

Has your faith been put to the test yet? If so, then you know that with God's help, you can endure life's darker days. But if you have not yet faced the inevitable trials and tragedies of life-here-on-earth, don't worry: you will. And when your faith is put to the test, rest assured that God is perfectly willing—and always ready—to give you strength for the struggle.

A Book Unlike Any Other

Your word is a lamp for my feet and a light on my path.
PSALM 119:105 HCSB

God's Word is unlike any other book. The words of Matthew 4:4 remind us that, "Man shall not live by bread alone but by every word that proceedeth out of the mouth of God" (KJV). As believers, we are instructed to study the Bible and meditate upon its meaning for our lives, yet far too many Bibles are laid aside by well-intentioned believers who would like to study the Bible if they could "just find the time."

Warren Wiersbe observed, "When the child of God looks into the Word of God, he sees the Son of God. And, he is transformed by the Spirit of God to share in the glory of God." God's Holy Word is, indeed, a transforming, life-changing, one-of-a-kind treasure. And it's up to you—and only you—to use it that way.

The balance of affirmation and discipline, freedom and restraint, encouragement and warning is different for each child and season and generation, yet the absolutes of God's Word are necessary and trustworthy no matter how mercuric the time.

GLORIA GAITHER

Integrity: It's Always the Right Way

People with integrity have firm footing, but those who follow crooked paths will slip and fall.

PROVERBS 10:9 NLT

Wise women understand that integrity is a crucial building block in the foundation of a well-lived life. Character is a precious thing—difficult to build, but easy to tear down. Godly women value it and protect it at all costs.

As believers in Christ, you must seek to live each day with discipline, honesty, and faith. When you do, at least two things happen: integrity will become a habit, and God will most certainly bless you because of your obedience to Him.

Living a life of integrity isn't always the easiest way, but it is always the right way. And God clearly intends that it should be your way, too. So if you find yourself tempted to break the truth—or even to bend it—remember that honesty is God's policy . . . and it must be yours.

God never called us to naïveté. He called us to integrity.... The biblical concept of integrity emphasizes mature innocence not childlike ignorance.

BETH MOORE

A Clear Conscience

I will maintain my righteousness and never let go of it; my conscience will not reproach me as long as I live.

JOB 27:6 NIV

A clear conscience is one of the many rewards you earn when you obey God's Word and follow His will. Whenever you know that you've done the right thing, you feel better about yourself, your life, and your future. A guilty conscience, on the other hand, is, for most people, it's own punishment.

In order to keep your conscience clear, you should study God's Word and obey it—you should seek God's will and follow it—you should honor God's Son and walk with Him. When you do, your earthly rewards are never-ceasing, and your heavenly rewards are everlasting.

God desires that we become spiritually healthy enough through faith to have a conscience that rightly interprets the work of the Holy Spirit.

BETH MOORE

Whatever weakens your reason, impairs the tenderness of your conscience, obscures your sense of God, or removes your relish for spiritual things—that is sin to you.

SUSANNA WESLEY

Making the Right Choices

*The Lord says, "I will make you wise and show you where
to go. I will guide you and watch over you."*

PSALM 32:8 NCV

Are you facing a tough decision that has you totally
confused? If so, here's a simple formula for making
the right choice: let God decide. Instead of fretting
about your future, pray about it.

When you consult your heavenly Father early and
often, you'll soon discover that God keeps His promises.
He has promised to lead you, to protect you, and guide
you—and that's precisely what He will do. In time, God
will quietly lead you along a path of His choosing, a
path that is right for you.

So the next time you arrive at one of life's inevitable
crossroads, consult God's roadmap (the Bible) and seek
God's guidance (in prayer). When you do, you'll never
stay lost for long.

There may be no trumpet sound or loud applause when
we make a right decision, just a calm sense of resolution
and peace.

GLORIA GAITHER

Meeting the Obligations

In all the work you are doing, work the best you can. Work as if you were doing it for the Lord, not for people.

COLOSSIANS 3:23 NCV

Nobody needs to tell you the obvious: You have lots of responsibilities—obligations to yourself, to your family, to your community, and to your God. And which of these duties should take priority? The answer can be found in Matthew 6:33: "But seek first the kingdom of God and His righteousness, and all these things will be provided for you" (HCSB).

When you "seek first the kingdom of God," all your other obligations have a way of falling into place. When you obey God's Word and seek His will, your many responsibilities don't seem quite so burdensome. When you honor God with your time, your talents. and your prayers, you'll be much more likely to count your blessings instead of your troubles.

So do yourself and your loved ones a favor: take all your duties seriously, especially your duties to God. When you do, you'll discover that pleasing your Father in heaven isn't just the right thing to do; it's also the best way to live.

God Protects

I know whom I have believed, and am convinced that he is able to guard what I have entrusted to him for that day.

2 TIMOTHY 1:12 NIV

God is willing to protect us. We, in turn, must open ourselves to His protection and His love. This point is illustrated by the familiar story found in the 4th chapter of Mark: When a terrible storm rose quickly on the Sea of Galilee, the disciples were afraid. Although they had witnessed many miracles, the disciples feared for their lives, so they turned to Jesus, and He calmed the waters and the wind.

Sometimes, we, like the disciples, feel threatened by the storms of life. And when we are fearful, we, too, can turn to Christ for comfort and for courage. The next time you find yourself facing a fear-provoking situation, remember that the One who calmed the wind and the waves is also your personal Savior. Then ask yourself which is stronger: your faith or your fear. The answer, friends, should be obvious: Whatever your challenge, God can handle it. Let Him.

Freely Give

If you give, you will receive. Your gift will return to you in full measure, pressed down, shaken together to make room for more, and running over. Whatever measure you use in giving—large or small—it will be used to measure what is given back to you.

LUKE 6:38 NLT

The words are familiar to those who study God's Word: "Freely you have received, freely give" (Matthew 10:8 NKJV). As followers of Christ, we have been given so much by God. In return, we must give freely of our time, our possessions, our testimonies, and our love.

Your salvation was earned at a terrible price: Christ gave His life for you on the cross at Calvary. Christ's gift is priceless, yet when you accept Jesus as your personal Savior, His gift of eternal life costs you nothing. From those to whom much has been given, much is required. And because you have received the gift of salvation, you are now called by God to be a cheerful, generous steward of the gifts He has placed under your care.

Today and every day, let Christ's words be your guide and let His eternal love fill your heart. When you do, your stewardship will be a reflection of your love for Him, and that's exactly as it should be.

His Comforting Hand

When I am filled with cares, Your comfort brings me joy.
PSALM 94:19 HCSB

As Christians, we can be assured of this fact: Whether we find ourselves on the pinnacle of the mountain or in the darkest depths of the valley, God is there.

If you have been touched by the transforming hand of Jesus, then you have every reason to live courageously. After all, Christ has already won the ultimate battle— and He won it for you—on the cross at Calvary.

The next time you find your courage tested to the limit, lean upon God's promises. Trust His Son. Remember that God is always near and that He is your protector and your deliverer. When you are worried, anxious, or afraid, call upon Him and accept the touch of His comforting hand. Remember that God rules both mountaintops and valleys—with limitless wisdom and love—now and forever.

When God allows extraordinary trials for His people, He prepares extraordinary comforts for them.

CORRIE TEN BOOM

He Is Love

God is love, and the one who remains in love remains in God, and God remains in him.

1 JOHN 4:16 HCSB

God is love. It's a sweeping statement, a profoundly important description of what God is and how God works. God's love is perfect. When we open our hearts to His perfect love, we are touched by the Creator's hand, and we are transformed.

Barbara Johnson observed, "We cannot protect ourselves from trouble, but we can dance through the puddles of life with a rainbow smile, twirling the only umbrella we need—the umbrella of God's love."

And the English mystical writer Juliana of Norwich noted, "We are so preciously loved by God that we cannot even comprehend it. No created being can ever know how much and how sweetly and tenderly God loves them."

So today, even if you can only carve out a few quiet moments, offer sincere prayers of thanksgiving to your Father. Thank Him for His blessings and His love.

His Will Be Done

Our Father which art in heaven, Hallowed be thy name. Thy kingdom come, Thy will be done in earth, as it is in heaven.

MATTHEW 6:9-10 KJV

When Jesus went to the Mount of Olives, as described in Luke 22, He poured out His heart to God. Jesus knew of the agony that He was destined to endure, but He also knew that God's will must be done. We, like our Savior, face trials that bring fear and trembling to the very depths of our souls, but like Christ, we, too, must ultimately seek God's will, not our own.

God has a plan for all our lives, but He will not force His plans upon us. To the contrary, He only makes His plans clear to those who genuinely and humbly seek His will. As this day unfolds, let us seek God's will and obey His Word. When we entrust our lives to Him completely and without reservation, He gives us the strength to meet any challenge, the courage to face any trial, and the wisdom to live in His righteousness and in His peace.

If my life is surrendered to God, all is well. Let me not grab it back, as though it were in peril in His hand but would be safer in mine!

ELISABETH ELLIOT

Beyond Guilt

Your beliefs about these things should be kept secret between you and God. People are happy if they can do what they think is right without feeling guilty.

ROMANS 14:22 NCV

All of us have made mistakes. Sometimes our failures result from our own shortsightedness. On other occasions, we are swept up in events that are beyond our abilities to control. Under either set of circumstances, we may experience intense feelings of guilt. But God has an answer for the guilt that we feel. That answer, of course, is His forgiveness.

When we ask our Heavenly Father for His forgiveness, He forgives us completely and without reservation. Then, we must do the difficult work of forgiving ourselves in the same way that God has forgiven us: thoroughly and unconditionally.

If you're feeling guilty, then it's time for a special kind of housecleaning—a housecleaning of your mind and your heart . . . beginning NOW!

One of Satan's most effective ploys is to make us believe that we are small, insignificant, and worthless.

SUSAN LENZKES

Look for the Joy

You will show me the way of life, granting me the joy of your presence and the pleasures of living with you forever.
PSALM 16:11 NLT

Barbara Johnson says, "You have to look for the joy. Look for the light of God that is hitting your life, and you will find sparkles you didn't know were there."

Have you experienced that kind of joy? Hopefully so, because it's not enough to hear someone else talk about being joyful—you must actually experience that kind of joy in order to understand it.

Should you expect to be a joy-filled woman 24 hours a day, seven days a week, from this moment on? No. But you can (and should) experience pockets of joy frequently—that's the kind of joy-filled life that a woman like you deserves to live.

Among the most joyful people I have known have been some who seem to have had no human reason for joy. The sweet fragrance of Christ has shown through their lives.

ELISABETH ELLIOT

Looking for Miracles

Depend on the Lord and his strength; always go to him for help. Remember the miracles he has done; remember his wonders and his decisions.

PSALM 105:4-5 NCV

If you haven't seen any of God's miracles lately, you haven't been looking. Throughout history the Creator has intervened in the course of human events in ways that cannot be explained by science or human rationale. And he's still doing so today.

God's miracles are not limited to special occasions, nor are they witnessed by a select few. God is crafting His wonders all around us: the miracle of the birth of a new baby; the miracle of a world renewing itself with every sunrise; the miracle of lives transformed by God's love and grace. Each day, God's handiwork is evident for all to see and experience.

Today, seize the opportunity to inspect God's hand at work. His miracles come in a variety of shapes and sizes, so keep your eyes and your heart open. Be watchful, and you'll soon be amazed.

I could go through this day oblivious to the miracles all around me or I could tune in and "enjoy."

GLORIA GAITHER

Passion for Life

Never be lacking in zeal, but keep your spiritual fervor, serving the Lord.

ROMANS 12:11 NIV

Are you passionate about your life, your loved ones, your work, and your faith? As a believer who has been saved by a risen Christ, you should be.

As a thoughtful Christian, you have every reason to be enthusiastic about life, but sometimes the struggles of everyday living may cause you to feel decidedly unenthusiastic. If you feel that your zest for life is slowly fading away, it's time to slow down, to rest, to count your blessings, and to pray. When you feel worried or weary, you must pray fervently for God to renew your sense of wonderment and excitement.

Life with God is a glorious adventure; revel in it. When you do, God will most certainly smile upon your work and your life.

Wouldn't it make astounding difference, not only in the quality of the work we do, but also in the satisfaction, even our joy, if we recognized God's gracious gift in every single task?

ELISABETH ELLIOT

Pleasing God

But neither exile nor homecoming is the main thing.
Cheerfully pleasing God is the main thing, and that's
what we aim to do, regardless of our conditions.

2 CORINTHIANS 5:9 MSG

Sometimes, because you're an imperfect human being, you may become so wrapped up in meeting society's expectations that you fail to focus on God's expectations. To do so is a mistake of major proportions—don't make it. Instead, seek God's guidance as you focus your energies on becoming the best "you" that you can possibly be. And, when it comes to matters of conscience, seek approval not from your peers, but from your Creator.

Who will you try to please today: God or man? Your primary obligation is not to please imperfect men and women. Your obligation is to strive diligently to meet the expectations of an all-knowing and perfect God. Trust Him always. Love Him always. Praise Him always. And seek to please Him. Always.

Get ready for God to show you not only His pleasure, but His approval.

JONI EARECKSON TADA

Real Prosperity

Serving God does make us very rich, if we are satisfied with what we have. We brought nothing into the world, so we can take nothing out. But, if we have food and clothes, we will be satisfied with that.

1 TIMOTHY 6:6-8 NCV

We live in an era of prosperity, a time when many of us have been richly blessed with an assortment of material possessions that our forebears could have scarcely imagined. As believers living in these prosperous times, we must be cautious: we must keep prosperity in perspective.

The world stresses the importance of material possessions; God does not. The world offers the promise of happiness through wealth and public acclaim; God offers the promise of peace through His Son. When in doubt, we must distrust the world and trust God. The world often makes promises that it cannot keep, but when God makes a promise, He keeps it, not just for a day or a year or a lifetime, for all eternity.

Our ultimate aim in life is not to be healthy, wealthy, prosperous, or problem free. Our ultimate aim in life is to bring glory to God.

ANNE GRAHAM LOTZ

Prayer Changes Things and You

*And everything—whatever you ask in prayer, believing—
you will receive.*

MATTHEW 21:22 HCSB

Is prayer an integral part of your daily life or is it a
hit-or-miss habit? Do you "pray without ceasing,"
or is your prayer life an afterthought? As you consider
the role that prayer currently plays in your life—and the
role that you think it should play—remember that the
quality of your spiritual life is inevitably related to the
quality of your prayer life.

Prayer changes things and it changes you. So today,
instead of turning things over in your mind, turn them
over to God in prayer. Instead of worrying about your
next decision, pray about it. Don't limit your prayers to
meals or to bedtime. Pray often about things great and
small. God is listening, and He wants to hear from you.
Now.

Our prayers must not be efforts to bend God to our will
but to yield ourselves to His.

CATHERINE MARSHALL

Your Bible and His Purpose

The words of the Lord are pure words, like silver tried in a furnace . . . .

PSALM 12:6 NKJV

Are you sincerely seeking to discover God's will and follow it? If so, study His Word and obey His commandments. The words of Matthew 4:4 remind us that, "Man shall not live by bread alone, but by every word that proceeds from the mouth of God." (NKJV). As believers, we must study the Bible and meditate upon its meaning for our lives. Otherwise, we deprive ourselves of a priceless gift from our Creator.

Jonathan Edwards advised, "Be assiduous in reading the Holy Scriptures. This is the fountain whence all knowledge in divinity must be derived. Therefore let not this treasure lie by you neglected." God's Holy Word is a priceless, one-of-a-kind treasure, and simply a passing acquaintance with the Good Book is insufficient for Christians who seek to obey God's Word and to understand His will.

Finding one's mission, and then fulfilling it, is perhaps the most vital activity in which a person can engage.

LAURIE BETH JONES

Repentance and Peace

They should repent, turn to God, and do works befitting repentance.

ACTS 26:20 NKJV

Who among us has sinned? All of us. But, God calls upon us to turn away from sin by following His commandments. And the good news is this: When we ask God's forgiveness and turn our hearts to Him, He forgives us absolutely and completely.

Genuine repentance requires more than simply offering God apologies for our misdeeds. Real repentance may start with feelings of sorrow and remorse, but it ends only when we turn away from the sin that has heretofore distanced us from our Creator. In truth, we offer our most meaningful apologies to God, not with our words, but with our actions. As long as we are still engaged in sin, we may be sorry but we have not fully "repented."

Is there an aspect of your life that is distancing you from your God and robbing you of His peace? If so, ask for His forgiveness, and—just as importantly—stop sinning. Then, wrap yourself in the protection of God's Word. When you do, you will be forgiven, you will be secure, and you will know peace.

Service and Love

We know we love God's children if we love God and obey his commandments.

1 JOHN 5:2 NLT

Jesus came to earth as a servant of man and the Savior of mankind. One way that we can demonstrate our love for the Savior is by obeying His commandment to serve one another.

Whom will you choose to serve today? Will you be a woman who cheerfully meets the needs of family and friends? And, will you meet those needs with love in your heart and encouragement on your lips? As you plan for the day ahead, remember that the needs are great and the workers are few. And remember that God is doing His very best to enlist able-bodied believers—like you.

Through our service to others, God wants to influence our world for Him.

VONETTE BRIGHT

A woman after God's own heart is a woman who carefully cultivates a servant's spirit.

ELIZABETH GEORGE

The Source of Strength

Have you not known? Have you not heard? The everlasting God, the Lord, the Creator of the ends of the earth, neither faints nor is weary. His understanding is unsearchable. He gives power to the weak, and to those who have no might He increases strength.

ISAIAH 40:28-29 NKJV

God is a never-ending source of strength and courage if we call upon Him. When we are weary, He gives us strength. When we see no hope, God reminds us of His promises. When we grieve, God wipes away our tears.

Do you feel overwhelmed by today's responsibilities? Do you feel pressured by the ever-increasing demands of 21st-century life? Then turn your concerns and your prayers over to God. He knows your needs, and He has promised to meet those needs. Whatever your circumstances, God will protect you and care for you... if you let Him. Invite Him into your heart and allow Him to renew you spirits. When you trust Him and Him alone, He will never fail you.

Focusing on His Blessings

Blessed is he whose help is the God of Jacob, whose hope is in the LORD his God, the Maker of heaven and earth, the sea, and everything in them—the LORD, who remains faithful forever.

PSALM 146:5-6 NIV

What is your focus today? Are you willing to focus your thoughts on the countless blessings that God has bestowed upon you? Before you answer that question, consider this: the direction of your thoughts will determine, to a surprising extent, the direction of your day and your life.

This day—and every day hereafter—is a chance to celebrate the life that God has given you. It's a chance to celebrate your relationships, your talents, and your opportunities. So focus your thoughts upon the gift of life—and upon the blessings that surround you.

You're a beautiful creation of God, a being of infinite importance. Give thanks for your gifts and share them. Never have the needs—or the opportunities for service—been greater.

Preoccupy my thoughts with your praise beginning today.

JONI EARECKSON TADA

Acceptance and Peace

Come to terms with God and be at peace; in this way good will come to you.

JOB 22:21 HCSB

All of us experience adversity and pain. As human beings with limited understanding, we can never fully understand the will of our Father in Heaven. But as believers in a benevolent God, we must always trust His providence.

When Jesus went to the Mount of Olives, He poured out His heart to God. Jesus knew of the agony that He was destined to endure, but He also knew that God's will must be done. We, like our Savior, must ultimately seek God's will, not our own.

Are you embittered by a personal tragedy that you did not deserve and cannot understand? If so, it's time to make peace with life. It's time to forgive others, and, if necessary, to forgive yourself. It's time to accept the unchangeable past, to embrace the priceless present, and to have faith in the promise of tomorrow. It's time to trust God completely. And it's time to reclaim the peace—His peace—that can and should be yours.

Asking Him for Strength

Keep asking, and it will be given to you. Keep searching, and you will find. Keep knocking, and the door will be opened to you. For everyone who asks receives, and the one who searches finds, and to the one who knocks, the door will be opened.

MATTHEW 7:7-8 HCSB

Are you a woman in need of renewal? Ask God to strengthen you. Are you troubled? Take your concerns to Him in prayer. Are you discouraged? Seek the comfort of God's promises. Do you feel trapped in a life that lacks fulfillment and joy? Ask God where He wants you to go, and then go there. In all things great and small, seek the transforming power of God's grace. He hears your prayers, and He will answer.

God makes prayer as easy as possible for us. He's completely approachable and available, and He'll never mock or upbraid us for bringing our needs before Him.

SHIRLEY DOBSON

You pay God a compliment by asking great things of Him.

ST. TERESA OF AVILA

His Compassion

For thou, LORD, wilt bless the righteous....

PSALM 5:12 KJV

Psalm 145 makes this promise: "The LORD is gracious and compassionate, slow to anger and rich in love. The LORD is good to all; he has compassion on all he has made" (8-9 NIV). As God's children, we are blessed beyond measure, but sometimes, as busy women in a demanding world, we are slow to count our gifts and even slower to give thanks to the Giver. Our blessings include life and health, family and friends, freedom and possessions—for starters. And, the gifts we receive from God are multiplied when we share them with others. May we always give thanks to God for our blessings, and may we always demonstrate our gratitude by sharing them.

We do not need to beg Him to bless us; He simply cannot help it.

HANNAH WHITALL SMITH

The Bible plainly teaches that if we will learn and act on the Word, God will bless our lives.

JOYCE MEYER

Making Quality Choices

I am offering you life or death, blessings or curses. Now, choose life! . . . To choose life is to love the Lord your God, obey him, and stay close to him.

DEUTERONOMY 30:19-20 NCV

Every life, including yours, is a tapestry of choices. And the quality of your life depends, to a surprising extent, on the quality of the choices you make.

Would you like to enjoy a life of abundance and significance? If so, you must make choices that are pleasing to God.

From the instant you wake up in the morning until the moment you nod off to sleep at night, you make lots of decisions: decisions about the things you do, decisions about the words you speak, and decisions about the thoughts you choose to think.

Today and every day, it's up to you (and only you) to make wise choices, choices that enhance your relationship with God. After all, He deserves no less than your best . . . and so do you.

Freedom is not the right to do what we want but the power to do what we ought.

CORRIE TEN BOOM

Living Courageously

So do not fear, for I am with you; do not be dismayed, for I am your God. I will strengthen you and help you; I will uphold you with my righteous right hand.

ISAIAH 41:10 NIV

Christian women have every reason to live courageously. After all, the final battle has already been won on the cross at Calvary. But even dedicated followers of Christ may find their courage tested by the inevitable disappointments and fears that visit the lives of believers and non-believers alike.

When you find yourself worried about the challenges of today or the uncertainties of tomorrow, you must ask yourself whether or not you are ready to place your concerns and your life in God's all-powerful, all-knowing, all-loving hands. If the answer to that question is yes—as it should be—then you can draw courage today from the source of strength that never fails: your Heavenly Father.

What is courage? It is the ability to be strong in trust, in conviction, in obedience. To be courageous is to step out in faith—to trust and obey, no matter what.

KAY ARTHUR

He Doesn't Fail

The LORD is my strength and my song; he has become my victory. He is my God, and I will praise him.

EXODUS 15:2 NLT

When we fail to meet the expectations of others (or, for that matter, the expectations that we have set for ourselves), we may be tempted to abandon hope. Thankfully, on those cloudy days when our strength is sapped and our faith is shaken, there exists God from whom we can draw courage and wisdom.

The words of Isaiah 40:31 teach us that, "Those who wait on the Lord shall renew their strength; They shall mount up with wings like eagles, They shall run and not be weary, They shall walk and not faint" (NKJV).

So if you're feeling defeated or discouraged, think again. And while you're thinking, consider the following advice from Mrs. Charles E. Cowman: "Never yield to gloomy anticipation. Place your hope and confidence in God. He has no record of failure."

The truth is that even in the midst of trouble, happy moments swim by us every day, like shining fish waiting to be caught.

BARBARA JOHNSON

Mountain-moving Faith

I assure you: If anyone says to this mountain, 'Be lifted up and thrown into the sea,' and does not doubt in his heart, but believes that what he says will happen, it will be done for him.

MARK 11:23 HCSB

Have you ever felt your faith in God slipping away? If so, you are not alone. Every life—including yours—is a series of successes and failures, celebrations and disappointments, joys and sorrows. But even when we feel very distant from God, God is never distant from us.

Jesus taught His disciples that if they had faith, they could move mountains. You can too. When you place your faith, your trust, indeed your life in the hands of Christ Jesus, you'll be amazed at the marvelous things He can do with you and through you. So strengthen your faith through praise, through worship, through Bible study, and through prayer. And trust God's plans. With Him, all things are possible, and He stands ready to open a world of possibilities to you if you have faith.

The Commandment to Forgive

Be merciful, just as your Father also is merciful.
LUKE 6:36 HCSB

Forgiving other people is hard—sometimes very hard. But God tells us that we must forgive others, even when we'd rather not. So, if you're angry with anybody (or if you're upset by something you yourself have done) it's time to forgive . . . now!

Life would be much simpler if you could forgive people "once and for all" and be done with it. Yet forgiveness is seldom that easy. Usually, the decision to forgive is straightforward, but the process of forgiving is more difficult. Forgiveness is a journey that requires effort, time, perseverance, and prayer.

God instructs you to treat other people exactly as you wish to be treated. And since you want to be forgiven for the mistakes that you make, you must be willing to extend forgiveness to other people for the mistakes that they have made. If you can't seem to forgive someone, you should keep asking God to help you until you do. And you can be sure of this: if you keep asking for God's help, He will give it.

Don't put a question mark where God put a period.
ANONYMOUS

His Perfection

For I will proclaim the Lord's name. Declare the greatness of our God! The Rock—His work is perfect; all His ways are entirely just. A faithful God, without prejudice, He is righteous and true.

DEUTERONOMY 32:3-4 HCSB

The hand of God is perfect. God is the Creator of life, the Sustainer of life, and the Rock upon which righteous lives are built. God is a never-ending source of support for those who trust Him, and He is a never-ending source of wisdom for those who study His Holy Word.

Is God the Rock upon which you've constructed your own life? If so, then you have chosen wisely. Your faith will give you the inner strength you need to rise above the inevitable demands and struggles of life.

God will hold your hand and walk with you today and every day if you let Him. Even if your circumstances are difficult, trust the Father. His promises remain true; His plan is perfect; His love is eternal; and His goodness endures forever.

The whole earth is full of His glory; Holy is the Lord.

NOLENE PRINCE

His Grace Is Not Earned

For by grace you are saved through faith, and this is not from yourselves; it is God's gift—not from works, so that no one can boast.

EPHESIANS 2:8-9 HCSB

God's grace is not earned . . . thank goodness! To earn God's love and His gift of eternal life would be far beyond the abilities of even the most righteous man or woman. Thankfully, grace is not an earthly reward for righteous behavior; it is a blessed spiritual gift which can be accepted by believers who dedicate themselves to God through Christ. When we accept Christ into our hearts, we are saved by His grace.

The familiar words of Ephesians 2:8 make God's promise perfectly clear: It is by grace we have been saved, through faith. We are saved not because of our good deeds but because of our faith in Christ.

Let us praise the Creator for His priceless gift, and let us share the Good News with all who cross our paths. We return our Father's love by accepting His grace and by sharing His message and His love. When we do, we are eternally blessed . . . and the Father smiles.

God's Armor

Finally, be strong in the Lord and in his mighty power. Put on the full armor of God so that you can take your stand against the devil's schemes.

EPHESIANS 6:10-11 NIV

In a world filled with dangers and temptations, God is the ultimate armor. In a world filled with misleading messages, God's Word is the ultimate truth. In a world filled with more frustrations than we can count, God's Son offers the ultimate peace. Will you accept God's peace and wear God's armor against the dangers of our world?

Sometimes, in the crush of everyday life, God may seem far away, but He is not. God is everywhere you have ever been and everywhere you will ever go. He is with you night and day; He knows your thoughts and your prayers. His is your ultimate Protector. And, when you earnestly seek His protection, you will find it because He is here—always—waiting patiently for you to reach out to Him.

He is within and without. His Spirit dwells within me. His armor protects me. He goes before me and is behind me.

MARY MORRISON SUGGS

Honoring God

Honor the Lord with your possessions, and with the firstfruits of all your increase; so your barns will be filled with plenty.

PROVERBS 3:9-10 NKJV

Whom will you choose to honor today? If you honor God and place Him at the center of your life, every day is a cause for celebration. But if you fail to honor your Heavenly Father, you're asking for trouble, and lots of it.

At times, your life is probably hectic, demanding, and complicated. When the demands of life leave you rushing from place to place with scarcely a moment to spare, you may fail to pause and thank your Creator for the blessings He has bestowed upon you. But that's a big mistake.

Do you sincerely seek to be a worthy servant of the One who has given you eternal love and eternal life? Then honor Him for who He is and for what He has done for you. And don't just honor Him on Sunday morning. Praise Him all day long, every day, for as long as you live . . . and then for all eternity.

Life Triumphant

*Shout triumphantly to the Lord, all the earth. Serve the
Lord with gladness; come before Him with joyful songs.*
PSALM 100:1-2 HCSB

Are you living the triumphant life that God
has promised? Or are you, instead, a spiritual
shrinking violet? As you ponder that question, consider
this: God does not intend that you live a life that is
commonplace or mediocre. And He doesn't want you
to hide your light "under a basket." Instead, He wants
you to "Let your light so shine before men, that they
may see your good works and glorify your Father in
heaven" (Matthew 5:16 NKJV). In short, God wants
you to live a triumphant life so that others might know
precisely what it means to be a believer.

The Christian life should be a triumphal celebration,
a daily exercise in thanksgiving and praise. Join that
celebration today. And while you're at it, make sure that
you let others know that you've joined.

Shout the shout of faith. Nothing can withstand the
triumphant faith that links itself to omnipotence. For
"this is the victory that overcometh the world." The
secret of all successful living lies in this shout of faith.
HANNAH WHITALL SMITH

Unchanging Laws

God's Law is more real and lasting than the stars in the sky and the ground at your feet. Long after stars burn out and earth wears out, God's Law will be alive and working.

MATTHEW 5:18 MSG

God's laws are eternal and unchanging: obedience leads to abundance and joy; disobedience leads to disaster. God has given us a guidebook for righteous living called the Holy Bible. If we trust God's Word and live by it, we are blessed. But, if we choose to ignore God's commandments, the results are as predictable as they are tragic.

When we live according to God's commandments, we earn for ourselves the abundance and peace that He intends for our lives.

Do you seek God's peace and His blessings? Then obey Him. When you're faced with a difficult choice or a powerful temptation, seek God's counsel and trust the counsel He gives. Invite God into your heart and live according to His commandments. When you do, you will be blessed today, and tomorrow, and forever.

Wait for Him

The Lord is wonderfully good to those who wait for him and seek him. So it is good to wait quietly for salvation from the Lord.

LAMENTATIONS 3:25-26 NLT

Are you a woman in a hurry? If so, you may be in for a few disappointments. Why? Because life has a way of unfolding according to its own timetable, not yours. That's why life requires patience . . . and lots of it!

Lamentations 3:25 reminds us that, "The Lord is wonderfully good to those who wait for him and seek him." (NIV). But, for most of us, waiting quietly is difficult because we're in such a hurry for things to happen!

The next time you find your patience tested to the limit, slow down, take a deep breath, and relax. Sometimes life can't be hurried—and during those times, patience is indeed a priceless virtue.

No matter what we are going through, no matter how long the waiting for answers, of one thing we may be sure. God is faithful. He keeps His promises. What he starts, He finishes...including His perfect work in us.

GLORIA GAITHER

Worship Every Day

Every day will I bless thee; and I will praise thy name for ever and ever.

PSALM 145:2 KJV

Too many of us, even well-intentioned believers, tend to "compartmentalize" our waking hours into a few familiar categories: work, rest, play, family time, and worship. As creatures of habit, we may find ourselves praising God only at particular times of the day or the week. But praise for our Creator should never be reserved for mealtimes, or bedtimes, or church. Instead, we should praise God all day, every day, to the greatest extent we can, with thanksgiving in our hearts, and with a song on our lips.

Worship and praise should be woven into the fabric of everything we do; they should not be relegated to a weekly three-hour visit to church on Sunday morning. A. W. Tozer correctly observed, "If you will not worship God seven days a week, you do not worship Him on one day a week."

Today, find a little more time to lift your prayers to God, and thank Him for all that He has done. Every time you notice a gift from the Giver of all things good, praise Him. His works are marvelous, His gifts are beyond understanding, and His love endures forever.

Pray Without Ceasing

Anyone who is having troubles should pray.

JAMES 5:13 NCV

In his first letter to the Thessalonians, Paul advised members of the new church to "pray without ceasing" (5:16-18). His advice applies to Christians of every generation. When we consult God on an hourly basis, we avail ourselves of His wisdom, His strength, and His love. As Corrie ten Boom observed, "Any concern that is too small to be turned into a prayer is too small to be made into a burden."

Today, instead of turning things over in your mind, turn them over to God in prayer. Instead of worrying about your next decision, ask God to lead the way. Don't limit your prayers to meals or bedtime. Become a woman of constant prayer. God is listening, and He wants to hear from you. Now.

The best reason to pray is that God is really there. In praying, our unbelief gradually starts to melt as God moves smack into the middle of even an ordinary day.

EMILIE GRIFFIN

Getting Past the Regrets

And don't be wishing you were someplace else or with someone else. Where you are right now is God's place for you. Live and obey and love and believe right there.

1 Corinthians 7:17 MSG

Bitterness can destroy you if you let it . . . so don't let it!

If you are caught up in intense feelings of anger or regret, you know all too well the destructive power of these emotions. How can you rid yourself of these feelings? First, you must prayerfully ask God to free you from these feelings. Then, you must learn to catch yourself whenever thoughts of bitterness begin to attack you. Your challenge is this: You must learn to resist negative thoughts before they hijack your emotions.

Christina Rossetti had this sound advice: "Better by far you should forget and smile than you should remember and be sad." And she was right—it's better to forget than regret.

We will always experience regret when we live for the moment and do not weigh our words and deeds before we give them life.

Lisa Bevere

If He Returned Today

But the Day of the Lord will come like a thief; on that day the heavens will pass away with a loud noise, the elements will burn and be dissolved, and the earth and the works on it will be disclosed . . . . Therefore, dear friends, while you wait for these things, make every effort to be found in peace without spot or blemish before Him.

2 PETER 3:10,14 HCSB

When will our Lord return? The Bible clearly states that the day and the hour of Christ's return is known only to God. Therefore, we must conduct our lives as if He were returning today.

If Jesus were to return this instant, would you be ready? Would you be proud of your actions, your thoughts, your relationships, and your prayers? If not, you must face up to a harsh reality: even if Christ does not return to earth today, He may call you home today! And if He does so, you must be prepared.

Have you given your heart to the resurrected Savior? If the answer to that question is anything other than an unqualified yes, then accept Him as your personal Savior before you close this book.

When the trumpet sounds—I'm outta here!

ANONYMOUS

Spiritual Gifts

Pursue love and desire spiritual gifts.
1 CORINTHIANS 14:1 HCSB

All of us have spiritual gifts, and if we're wise, we continue to refine those gifts every day. The journey toward spiritual maturity lasts a lifetime. As Christians, we can and should continue to grow in the love and the knowledge of our Savior as long as we live. When we cease to grow, either emotionally or spiritually, we do ourselves a profound disservice. But, if we study God's Word, if we obey His commandments, and if we live in the center of His will, we will not be "stagnant" believers; we will, instead, be growing Christians . . . and that's exactly what God intends for us to be.

When we live according to the principles contained in God's Holy Word, we embark upon a journey of spiritual maturity that results in life abundant and life eternal.

Faith Tip:
Each person possesses special abilities that can
be nurtured carefully or ignored totally.
The challenge, of course, is to do the former
and to avoid the latter.

A World Filled with Temptations

Look straight ahead, and fix your eyes on what lies before you. Mark out a straight path for your feet; then stick to the path and stay safe. Don't get sidetracked; keep your feet from following evil.

PROVERBS 4:25-27 NLT

If you stop to think about it, the cold, hard evidence is right in front of your eyes: you live in a temptation-filled world. The devil is out on the street, hard at work, causing pain and heartache in more ways than ever before. Here in the 21st Century, the bad guys are working around the clock to lead you astray. That's why you must remain vigilant.

In a letter to believers, Peter offered a stern warning: "Your adversary, the devil, prowls around like a roaring lion, seeking someone to devour" (I Peter 5:8 NASB). What was true in New Testament times is equally true in our own. Satan tempts his prey and then devours them. As believing Christians, we must beware. And, if we seek righteousness in our own lives, we must earnestly wrap ourselves in the protection of God's Holy Word. When we do, we are secure.

Be Transformed

And do not be conformed to this world, but be transformed by the renewing of your mind, that you may prove what is that good and acceptable and perfect will of God.

ROMANS 12:2 NKJV

Believers who fashion their days around Jesus are transformed: They see the world differently; they act differently, and they feel differently about themselves and their neighbors.

Thoughtful believers face the inevitable challenges and disappointments of each day armed with the joy of Christ and the promise of salvation. So whatever this day holds for you, begin it and end it with God as your partner and Christ as your Savior. And throughout the day, give thanks to the One who created you and saved you. God's love for you is infinite. Accept it joyously and be thankful.

In the midst of the pressure and the heat, I am confident His hand is on my life, developing my faith until I display His glory, transforming me into a vessel of honor that pleases Him!

ANNE GRAHAM LOTZ

Walking with God

How happy is everyone who fears the Lord, who walks in His ways!

PSALM 128:1 HCSB

Are you tired? Discouraged? Fearful? Be comforted. Take a walk with God. Jesus called upon believers to walk with Him, and He promised them that He would teach them how to live freely and lightly (Matthew 11:28-30). Are you worried or anxious? Be confident in God's power. He will never desert you. Do you see no hope for the future? Be courageous and call upon God. He will protect you and then use you according to His purposes. Are you grieving? Know that God hears your suffering. He will comfort you and, in time, He will dry your tears. Are you confused? Listen to the quiet voice of your Heavenly Father. He is not a God of confusion. Talk with Him; listen to Him; follow His commandments. He is steadfast, and He is your Protector...forever.

You can't walk with God and hold hands with Satan at the same time.

ANONYMOUS

The Futility of Worry

Worry is a heavy load . . . .

PROVERBS 12:25 NCV

"Worry does not empty tomorrow of its sorrow; it empties today of its strength." So writes Corrie ten Boom, a woman who survived a Nazi concentration camp during World War II. And while our own situations cannot be compared to Corrie's, we still worry about countless matters both great and small. Even though we are Christians who have been given the assurance of salvation—even though we are Christians who have received the promise of God's love and protection—we find ourselves fretting over the countless details of everyday life. Jesus understood our concerns when he spoke the reassuring words found in Matthew 6: "Therefore I tell you, do not worry about your life . . ."

As you consider the promises of Jesus, remember that God still sits in His heaven and you are His beloved child. Then, perhaps, you will worry a little less and trust God a little more, and that's as it should be because God is trustworthy . . . and you are protected.

Submit each day to God, knowing that He is God over all your tomorrows.

KAY ARTHUR

The Peace That Passes All Understanding

Peace, peace to you, and peace to him who helps you, for your God helps you.

1 CHRONICLES 12:18 HCSB

Through His Son, God offers a "peace that passes all understanding," but He does not force His peace upon us. God's peace is a blessing that we, as children of a loving Father, must claim for ourselves . . . but sometimes we are slow to do so. Why? Because we are fallible human beings with limited understanding and limited faith.

Have you found the lasting peace that can be yours through Jesus, or are you still rushing after the illusion of "peace and happiness" that the world promises but cannot deliver?

Today, as a gift to yourself, to your family, and to your friends, claim the inner peace that is your spiritual birthright: the peace of Jesus Christ. It is offered freely; it has been paid for in full; it is yours for the asking. So ask. And then share.

Our soul can never have rest in things that are beneath itself.

JULIANA OF NORWICH

Who Deserves the Credit?

But God, who comforts the humble, comforted us . . . .
2 CORINTHIANS 7:6 HCSB

When we experience success, it's easy to proclaim, "I did that!" But it's wrong. Dietrich Bonhoeffer was correct when he observed, "It is very easy to overestimate the importance of our own achievements in comparison with what we owe others." In other words, reality breeds humility.

Who are the greatest among us? Are they the proud and the powerful? Hardly. The greatest among us are the humble servants who care less for their own glory and more for God's glory. If we seek greatness in God's eyes, we must forever praise God's good works, not our own.

If you're tempted to overestimate your own accomplishments, resist that temptation. Instead of puffing out your chest and saying, "Look at me!", give credit where credit is due, starting with God. And, rest assured: There is no such thing as a self-made man. All of us are made by God . . . and He deserves the glory, not us.

Acceptance Now

People may make plans in their minds, but the Lord decides what they will do.

PROVERBS 16:9 NCV

Sometimes, we must accept life on its terms, not our own. Life has a way of unfolding, not as we will, but as it will. And sometimes, there is precious little we can do to change things.

When events transpire that are beyond our control, we have a choice: we can either learn the art of acceptance, or we can make ourselves miserable as we struggle to change the unchangable.

We must entrust the things we cannot change to God. Once we have done so, we can prayerfully and faithfully tackle the important work that He has placed before us: doing something about the things we can change . . . and doing it sooner rather than later.

Part of waiting upon the Lord is telling God that you want only what He wants—whatever it is.

KAY ARTHUR

Loving Him means the thankful acceptance of all things that His love has appointed.

ELISABETH ELLIOT

Abundance, Not Anxiety

Therefore don't worry about tomorrow, because tomorrow will worry about itself. Each day has enough trouble of its own.

MATTHEW 6:34 HCSB

We live in a world that often breeds anxiety and fear. When we come face-to-face with tough times, we may fall prey to discouragement, doubt, or depression. But our Father in Heaven has other plans. God has promised that we may lead lives of abundance, not anxiety. In fact, His Word instructs us to "be anxious for nothing." But how can we put our fears to rest? By taking those fears to God and leaving them there.

As you face the challenges of everyday living, do you find yourself becoming anxious, troubled, discouraged, or fearful? If so, turn every one of your concerns over to your Heavenly Father. The same God who created the universe will comfort you if you ask Him . . . so ask Him and trust Him. And then watch in amazement as your anxieties melt into the warmth of His loving hands.

Worry is a cycle of inefficient thoughts whirling around a center of fear.

CORRIE TEN BOOM

Actions and Beliefs

If the way you live isn't consistent with what you believe, then it's wrong.

ROMANS 14:23 MSG

We must do our best to make sure that our actions are accurate reflections of our beliefs. Our theology must be demonstrated, not only by our words but, more importantly, by our actions. In short, we should be practical women, quick to act upon the beliefs that we hold most dear.

We may proclaim our beliefs to our hearts' content, but our proclamations will mean nothing—to others or to ourselves—unless we accompany our words with deeds that match. The sermons that we live are far more compelling than the ones we preach.

Like it or not, your life is an accurate reflection of your creed. If this fact gives you cause for concern, don't bother talking about the changes that you intend to make—make them. Now.

Jesus taught that the evidence that confirms our leaps of faith comes after we risk believing, not before.

GLORIA GAITHER

His Love Endures

But the love of the Lord remains forever with those who fear him. His salvation extends to the children's children of those who are faithful to his covenant, of those who obey his commandments!

PSALM 103:17-18 NLT

Are you anxious about situations that you cannot control? Take your anxieties to God. Are you troubled by changes that threaten to disrupt your life? Take your troubles to Him. Does your corner of the world seem to be shaking beneath your feet? Seek protection from the One who cannot be moved.

The same God who created the universe will protect you if you ask Him . . . so ask Him . . . and then serve Him with willing hands and a trusting heart. Rest assured that the world may change moment by moment, but God's love—a love that is unfathomable and unchanging—endures forever.

Conditions are always changing; therefore, I must not be dependent upon conditions. What matters supremely is my soul and my relationship to God.

CORRIE TEN BOOM

Trusting Your Conscience

Let us come near to God with a sincere heart and a sure faith, because we have been made free from a guilty conscience, and our bodies have been washed with pure water.

HEBREWS 10:22 NCV

It has been said that character is what we are when nobody is watching. How true. When we do things that we know aren't right, we try to hide them from our families and friends. But even then, God is watching.

Few things in life torment us more than a guilty conscience. And, few things in life provide more contentment than the knowledge that we are obeying the conscience that God has placed in our hearts.

If you sincerely want to create the best possible life for yourself and your loved ones, never forsake your conscience. And remember this: when you walk with God, your character will take care of itself . . . and you won't need to look over your shoulder to see who, besides God, is watching.

There is no pillow so soft as a clear conscience.

ANONYMOUS

When Solutions Aren't Easy

For God has not given us a spirit of fearfulness, but one of power, love, and sound judgment.

2 TIMOTHY 1:7 HCSB

Sometimes, we all face problems that defy easy solutions. If you find yourself facing a difficult decision, here's a simple formula for making the right choice: let God decide. Instead of fretting about your future, pray about it.

When you consult your heavenly Father early and often, you'll soon discover that the quiet moments you spend with God can be very helpful. Many times, God will quietly lead you along a path of His choosing, a path that is right for you.

So the next time you arrive at one of life's inevitable crossroads, take a moment or two to bow your head and have a chat with the Ultimate Advisor. When you do, you'll never stay lost for long.

When we learn to listen to Christ's voice for the details of our daily decisions, we begin to know Him personally.

CATHERINE MARSHALL

Opportunities to Encourage

So encourage each other and give each other strength, just as you are doing now.

1 THESSALONIANS 5:11 NCV

Here's a question only you can answer: During a typical day, how many opportunities will you have to encourage other human beings? Unless you're living on a deserted island, the answer is "a lot!" And here's a follow-up question: How often do you take advantage of those opportunities? Hopefully, the answer is "more often than not."

Romans 14:19 advises us to "Pursue what promotes peace and what builds up one another" (HCSB). And whenever we do, God smiles.

Whether you realize it or not, you're surrounded by people who need an encouraging word, a helping hand, or a pat on the back. And every time you encourage one of these folks, you'll being doing God's will by obeying God's Word. So with no further ado, let the encouragement begin.

A single word, if spoken in a friendly spirit, may be sufficient to turn one from dangerous error.

FANNY CROSBY

When Your Courage Is Tested

Be strong and courageous, all you who put your hope in the Lord.

PSALM 31:24 HCSB

Even the most dedicated Christian woman may find her courage tested by the inevitable disappointments and tragedies of life. After all, we live in a world filled with uncertainty, hardship, sickness, and danger. Old Man Trouble, it seems, is never too far from the front door.

When we focus upon our fears and our doubts, we may find many reasons to lie awake at night and fret about the uncertainties of the coming day. A better strategy, of course, is to focus not upon our fears, but instead upon our God.

God is as near as your next breath, and He is in control. He offers salvation to all His children, including you. God is your shield and your strength; you are His forever. So don't focus your thoughts upon the fears of the day. Instead, trust God's plan and His eternal love for you. And remember: whatever the size of your challenge, God is bigger.

Cheerful Generosity

So let each one give as he purposes in his heart, not grudgingly or of necessity; for God loves a cheerful giver.

2 CORINTHIANS 9:7 NKJV

A re you a cheerful giver? If you intend to obey God's commandments, you must be. When you give, God looks not only at the quality of your gift, but also at the condition of your heart. If you give generously, joyfully, and without complaint, you obey God's Word. But, if you make your gifts grudgingly, or if the motivation for your gift is selfish, you disobey your Creator, even if you have tithed in accordance with Biblical principles.

Today, take God's commandments to heart and make this pledge: Be a cheerful, generous, courageous giver. The world needs your help, and you need the spiritual rewards that will be yours when you give faithfully, prayerfully, and cheerfully.

A cheerful giver does not count the cost of what he gives. His heart is set on pleasing and cheering him to whom the gift is given.

JULIANA OF NORWICH

Obey and Be Blessed

Good people will have rich blessings, but the wicked will be overwhelmed . . . .

PROVERBS 10:6 NCV

God gave us His commandments for a reason: so that we might obey them and be blessed. Elisabeth Elliot advised, "Obedience to God is our job. The results of that obedience are God's." These words should serve to remind us that obedience is imperative. But, we live in a world that presents us with countless temptations to disobey God's laws.

When we stray from God's path, we suffer. So, whenever we are confronted with sin, we have clear instructions: we must walk—or better yet run—in the opposite direction.

Obedience is a foundational stepping stone on the path of God's Will.

ELIZABETH GEORGE

Perfect obedience would be perfect happiness, if only we had perfect confidence in the power we were obeying.

CORRIE TEN BOOM

Our Merciful Father

You know the Lord is full of mercy and is kind.

God's hand offers forgiveness and salvation. God's mercy, like His love, is infinite and everlasting—it knows no boundaries. As a demonstration of His mercy, God sent His only Son to die for our sins, and we must praise our Creator for that priceless gift.

Romans 3:23 reminds us of a universal truth: "All have sinned, and come short of the glory of God" (KJV). All of us, even the most righteous among us, are sinners. But despite our imperfections, our merciful Father in heaven offers us salvation through the person of His Son.

As Christians, we have been blessed by a merciful, loving God. May we accept His mercy. And may we, in turn, show love and mercy to our friends, to our families, and to all whom He chooses to place along our paths.

Because his mercies are new every morning, you can find the courage to bring all of who you are to all of who he is.

SHEILA WALSH

Following His Plan

The counsel of the LORD stands forever, the plans of His heart from generation to generation.

PSALM 33:11 NASB

You can expect a satisfying and fulfilling life when you follow God's plan for your life. But how can you discern God's will? You should begin by studying God's Word and obeying His commandments. You should watch carefully for His signs, and you should associate with fellow Christians who encourage your spiritual growth. And you should listen to that inner voice that speaks to you in the quiet moments of your daily devotionals.

God intends to use you in wonderful, unexpected ways if you let Him. The decision to seek God's plan and to follow it is yours and yours alone. The consequences of that decision have implications that are both profound and eternal, so choose carefully.

The cross that Jesus commands you and me to carry is the cross of submissive obedience to the will of God, even when His will includes suffering and hardship and things we don't want to do.

ANNE GRAHAM LOTZ

The Power of Habits

Do not be deceived: "Evil company corrupts good habits."
1 CORINTHIANS 15:33 NKJV

It's an old saying and a true one: First, you make your habits, and then your habits make you. Some habits will inevitably bring you closer to God; other habits will lead you away from the path He has chosen for you. If you sincerely desire to improve your spiritual health, you must honestly examine the habits that make up the fabric of your day. And you must abandon those habits that are displeasing to God.

If you trust God, and if you keep asking for His help, He can transform your life. If you sincerely ask Him to help you, the same God who created the universe will help you defeat the harmful habits that have heretofore defeated you. So, if at first you don't succeed, keep praying. God is listening, and He's ready to help you become a better person if you ask Him . . . so ask today.

If you want to form a new habit, get to work. If you want to break a bad habit, get on your knees.

MARIE T. FREEMAN

Share His Joy

The Lord reigns; Let the earth rejoice.

PSALM 97:1 NKJV

God intends that all Christians should share His love with His joy in their hearts. But sometimes, in the hustle and bustle of our daily lives, we can forfeit—temporarily—God's joy as we wrestle with the challenges of daily living.

Joni Eareckson Tada spoke for Christian women of every generation when she observed, "I wanted the deepest part of me to vibrate with that ancient yet familiar longing, that desire for something that would fill and overflow my soul."

If, today, your heart is heavy, open the door of your soul to Christ. He will give you peace and joy. And if you already have the joy of Christ in your heart, share it freely, just as Christ freely shared His joy with you.

Every morning is a fresh opportunity to find God's extraordinary joy in the most ordinary places.

JANET. L. WEAVER

Expect a Miracle

Looking at them, Jesus said, "With men it is impossible, but not with God, because all things are possible with God."

MARK 10:27 HCSB

When you invite Christ to rule over your heart, you avail yourself of His power. And make no mistake about it: You and Christ, working together, can do miraculous things. In fact, miraculous things are exactly what Christ intends for you to do, but He won't force you to do great things on His behalf. The decision to become a full-fledged participant in His power is a decision that you must make for yourself.

Jesus made this promise: "I assure you: The one who believes in Me will also do the works that I do" (John 14:12 HCSB). In other words, when you put absolute faith in Christ, you can share in His power. So today, trust the Savior's promise—and expect a miracle in His name.

Faith means believing in realities that go beyond sense and sight. It is the awareness of unseen divine realities all around you.

JONI EARECKSON TADA

Passion and Purpose

May He grant you according to your heart's desire, and fulfill all your purpose.

PSALM 20:4 NKJV

We all need to discover a purpose for our lives, a purpose that excites us and causes us to live each day with passion.

Anna Quindlen had this advice: "Consider the lilies of the field. Look at the fuzz on a baby's ear. Read in the backyard with the sun on your face. Learn to be happy. And think of life as a terminal illness, because, if you do, you will live it with joy and passion, as it ought to be lived."

If you have not yet discovered a passionate pursuit that blesses you and your world, don't allow yourself to become discouraged. Instead, keep searching and keep trusting that with God's help, you can—and will—find a meaningful way to serve your neighbors, your Creator, and yourself.

One can never consent to creep when one feels an impulse to soar.

HELEN KELLER

His Perspective . . . and Yours

Since you have been raised to new life with Christ, set your sights on the realities of heaven, where Christ sits at God's right hand in the place of honor and power.

COLOSSIANS 3:1 NLT

If a temporary loss of perspective has left you worried, exhausted, or both, it's time to readjust your thought patterns. Negative thoughts are habit-forming; thankfully, so are positive ones. With practice, you can form the habit of focusing on God's priorities and your own possibilities. When you do, you'll soon discover that you will spend less time fretting about your challenges and more time praising God for His gifts.

When you call upon the Lord and prayerfully seek His will, He will give you wisdom and perspective. When you make God's priorities your priorities, He will direct your steps and calm your fears. So today and every day hereafter, pray for a sense of balance and perspective. And remember: no problems are too big for God—and that includes yours.

Instead of being frustrated and overwhelmed by all that is going on in our world, go to the Lord and ask Him to give you His eternal perspective.

KAY ARTHUR

Living in Our Material World

A pretentious, showy life is an empty life; a plain and simple life is a full life.

PROVERBS 13:7 MSG

On the grand stage of a well-lived life, material possessions should play a rather small role. Of course, we all need the basic necessities of life, but once we meet those needs for ourselves and for our families, the piling up of possessions creates more problems than it solves. Our real riches, of course, are not of this world. We are never really rich until we are rich in spirit.

Do you find yourself wrapped up in the concerns of the material world? If so, it's time to reorder your priorities by turning your thoughts and your prayers to more important matters. And, it's time to begin storing up riches that will endure throughout eternity: the spiritual kind.

When we put people before possessions in our hearts, we are sowing seeds of enduring satisfaction.

BEVERLY LAHAYE

I've learned to hold everything loosely because it hurts when God pries my fingers from it.

CORRIE TEN BOOM

The Antidote to Fear

I sought the LORD, and he heard me, and delivered me from all my fears.

PSALM 34:4 KJV

Considered by some to be the most popular cowgirl of time, she starred with cowboy husband Roy Rogers, and she wrote their theme song "Happy Trails." She was Dale Evans, and she said, "I have found the perfect antidote for fear. Whenever it sticks up its ugly face, I clobber it with prayer."

The Psalmist, we read, "In my distress I prayed to the LORD, and the LORD answered me and rescued me" (118:5). And He'll do the same for you. So if you've been beset by the inevitable disappointments and fears that grip us all from time to time, pray for courage and keep praying. When you, then like Dale Evans and Roy Rogers, you'll see plenty of clear skies and lots of happy trails.

Any concern that is too small to be turned into a prayer is too small to be made into a burden.

CORRIE TEN BOOM

Purpose Day by Day

Yet Lord, You are our Father; we are the clay, and You are our potter; we all are the work of Your hands.

ISAIAH 64:8 HCSB

Each morning, as the sun rises in the east, you welcome a new day, one that is filled to the brim with opportunities, with possibilities, and with God. As you contemplate God's blessings in your own life, you should prayerfully seek His guidance for the day ahead.

Discovering God's unfolding purpose for your life is a daily journey, a journey guided by the teachings of God's Holy Word. As you reflect upon God's promises and upon the meaning that those promises hold for you, ask God to lead you throughout the coming day. Let your Heavenly Father direct your steps; concentrate on what God wants you to do now, and leave the distant future in hands that are far more capable than your own: His hands.

Your job may be and ideally should be part of your mission, but a mission is always larger than a job. Jobs can change—and probably will.

LAURIE BETH JONES

Reaping His Rewards

The LORD approves of those who are good, but he condemns those who plan wickedness.

PROVERBS 12:2 NLT

When we seek righteousness in our own lives— and when we seek the companionship of those who do likewise—we reap the spiritual rewards that God intends for us to enjoy. When we behave ourselves as godly women, we honor God. When we live righteously and according to God's commandments, He blesses us in ways that we cannot fully understand.

You (and only you) are accountable for your actions. So hold fast that which is good, and associate yourself with believers who behave themselves in like fashion. When you do, your good works will serves as a powerful example for others and as a worthy offering to your Creator.

He doesn't need an abundance of words. He doesn't need a dissertation about your life. He just wants your attention. He wants your heart.

KATHY TROCCOLI

Spiritual Growth

Grow in grace and understanding of our Master and Savior, Jesus Christ. Glory to the Master, now and forever! Yes!

2 PETER 3:18 MSG

If we are to grow as Christians and as women, we need both knowledge and wisdom. Knowledge is found in textbooks. Wisdom, on the other hand, is found in God's Holy Word and in the carefully-chosen words of loving parents, family members, and friends. Knowledge is an important building block in a well-lived life, and it pays rich dividends both personally and professionally. But, wisdom is even more important because it refashions not only the mind, but also the heart.

When it comes to your faith, God doesn't intend for you to stand still. As a Christian, you should continue to grow in the love and the knowledge of your Savior as long as you live. How? By studying God's Word every day, by obeying His commandments, and by allowing His Son to reign over your heart.

Grace meets you where you are, but it doesn't leave you where it found you.

ANNE LAMOTT

Depending Upon God

Search for the Lord and for His strength; seek His face always.

PSALM 105:4-5 HCSB

God's love and support never changes. From the cradle to the grave, God has promised to give you the strength to meet any challenge. God has promised to lift you up and guide your steps if you let Him. God has promised that when you entrust your life to Him completely and without reservation, He will give you the courage to face any trial and the wisdom to live in His righteousness.

God's hand uplifts those who turn their hearts and prayers to Him. Will you count yourself among that number? Will you accept God's peace and wear God's armor against the temptations and distractions of our dangerous world? If you do, you can live courageously and optimistically, knowing that you have been forever touched by the loving, unfailing, uplifting hand of God.

Sometimes I think spiritual and physical strength is like manna: you get just what you need for the day, no more.

SUZANNE DALE EZELL

Beyond Pessimism

But we are hoping for something we do not have yet, and we are waiting for it patiently.

ROMANS 8:25 NCV

When you decided to allow Christ to rule over your heart, you entitled yourself to share in His promise of spiritual abundance and eternal joy. Have you claimed that entitlement? Are you an upbeat believer? Are you a person whose hopes and dreams are alive and well? Hopefully so. But sometimes, when pessimism and doubt invade your thoughts, you won't feel like celebrating. Why? Because thoughts are extremely powerful things.

If you've allowed pessimism to creep into your mind and heart, you should spend more time thinking about your blessings and less time fretting about your hardships. Then, you should take time to thank the Giver of all things good for gifts that are, in truth, far too numerous to count.

No more imperfect thoughts. No more sad memories. No more ignorance. My redeemed body will have a redeemed mind. Grant me a foretaste of that perfect mind as you mirror your thoughts in me today.

JONI EARECKSON TADA

Accepting Christ

We know very well that we are not set right with God by rule-keeping but only through personal faith in Jesus Christ.

GALATIANS 2:16 MSG

God's love for you is deeper and more profound than you can imagine. God's love for you is so great that He sent His only Son to this earth to die for your sins and to offer you the priceless gift of eternal life. Now, you must decide whether or not to accept God's gift. Will you ignore it or embrace it? Will you return it or neglect it? Will you accept Christ, or will you turn from Him?

Your decision to accept Christ is the pivotal decision of your life. It is a decision that you cannot ignore. It is a decision that is yours and yours alone. It is a decision with profound consequences, both earthly and eternal. Accept God's gift: Accept Christ today.

Choose Jesus Christ! Deny yourself, take up the Cross, and follow Him—for the world must be shown. The world must see, in us, a discernible, visible, startling difference.

ELISABETH ELLIOT

Ask Him

Ask in my name, according to my will, and he'll most certainly give it to you. Your joy will be a river overflowing its banks!

JOHN 16:24 MSG

God gives the gifts; we, as believers, should accept them—but oftentimes, we don't. Why? Because we fail to trust our Heavenly Father completely, and because we are, at times, surprisingly stubborn. Luke 11 teaches us that God does not withhold spiritual gifts from those who ask. Our obligation, quite simply, is to ask for them.

Are you a woman who asks God to move mountains in your life, or are you expecting Him to stumble over molehills? Whatever the size of your challenges, God is big enough to handle them. Ask for His help today, with faith and with fervor, and then watch in amazement as your mountains begin to move.

We get into trouble when we think we know what to do and we stop asking God if we're doing it.

STORMIE OMARTIAN

Counting Your Blessings

The Lord bless you and keep you; The Lord make His face shine upon you, And be gracious to you.

NUMBERS 6:24-25 NKJV

If you sat down and began counting your blessings, how long would it take? A very, very long time! Your blessings include life, freedom, family, friends, talents, and possessions, for starters. But, your greatest blessing—a gift that is yours for the asking—is God's gift of salvation through Christ Jesus.

Today, give thanks for your blessings by accepting them fully (with open arms) and by sharing them generously (with a thankful heart).

Billy Graham had this advice: "Think of the blessings we so easily take for granted: Life itself; preservation from danger; every bit of health we enjoy; every hour of liberty; the ability to see, to hear, to speak, to think, and to imagine all this comes from the hand of God." And that's sound advice for Christians—like you—who have been blessed beyond measure.

Oh! what a Savior, gracious to all, Oh! how His blessings round us fall, Gently to comfort, kindly to cheer, Sleeping or waking, God is near.

FANNY CROSBY

When It's Hard to Be Cheerful

Be cheerful. Keep things in good repair. Keep your spirits up. Think in harmony. Be agreeable. Do all that, and the God of love and peace will be with you for sure.

2 CORINTHIANS 13:11 MSG

On some days, as every woman knows, it's hard to be cheerful. Sometimes, as the demands of the world increase and our energy sags, we feel less like "cheering up" and more like "tearing up." But even in our darkest hours, we can turn to God, and He will give us comfort.

Christ promises us lives of abundance and joy, but He does not force this upon us. We must claim His abundance and His joy for ourselves, and when we do, Jesus, in turn, fills our spirits with His power and His love.

When we earnestly commit ourselves to the Savior of mankind, when we place Jesus at the center of our lives and trust Him as our personal Savior, He will transform us, not just for today, but for all eternity. Then we, as God's children, can share Christ's joy and His message with a world that needs both.

Beyond the Crises

But the wisdom that is from above is first pure, then peaceable, gentle, willing to yield, full of mercy and good fruits, without partiality and without hypocrisy.

JAMES 3:17 NKJV

Your decision to seek a deeper relationship with God will not remove all problems from your life; to the contrary, it will bring about a series of personal crises as you constantly seek to say "yes" to God although the world encourages you to do otherwise. You live in a world that seeks to snare your attention and lead you away from God. Each time you are tempted to distance yourself from the Creator, you will face a spiritual crisis. A few of these crises may be monumental in scope, but most will be the small, everyday decisions of life. In fact, life here on earth can be seen as one test after another—and with each crisis comes yet another opportunity to grow closer to God . . . or to distance yourself from His plan for your life.

Today, you will face many opportunities to say "yes" to your Creator—and you will also encounter many opportunities to say "no" to Him. Your answers will determine the quality of your day and the direction of your life, so answer carefully . . . very carefully.

When the Path is Dark

When doubts filled my mind, your comfort gave me renewed hope and cheer.

PSALM 94:19 NLT

Doubts come in several shapes and sizes: doubts about God, doubts about the future, and doubts about our own abilities, for starters. But when doubts creep in, as they will from time to time, we need not despair.

God never leaves our side, not for an instant. He is always with us, always willing to calm the storms of life. When we sincerely seek His presence—and when we genuinely seek to establish a deeper, more meaningful relationship Him—God is prepared to touch our hearts, to calm our fears, to answer our doubts, and to restore our confidence.

Dark as my path may seem to others, I carry a magic light in my heart. Faith, the spiritual strong searchlight, illumines the way, and although sinister doubts lurk in the shadow, I walk unafraid toward the enchanted wood where the foliage is always green, where joy abides, where nightingales nest and sing, and where life and death are one in the presence of the Lord.

HELEN KELLER

What Kind of Example?

You are the light that gives light to the world. In the same way, you should be a light for other people. Live so that they will see the good things you do and will praise your Father in heaven.

MATTHEW 5:14,16 NCV

Whether we like it or not, all of us are examples. The question is not whether we will be examples to our families and friends; the question is simply what kind of examples will we be.

What kind of example are you? Are you the kind of woman whose life serves as a powerful example of righteousness? Are you a woman whose behavior serves as a positive role model for young people? Are you the kind of woman whose actions, day in and day out, are based upon integrity, fidelity, and a love for the Lord? If so, you are not only blessed by God, you are also a powerful force for good in a world that desperately needs positive influences such as yours.

D. L. Moody advised, "A man ought to live so that everybody knows he is a Christian, and most of all, his family ought to know." And that's sound advice because our families and friends are watching . . . and so, for that matter, is God.

Forgive Everybody!

Be kind to one another, tender-hearted, forgiving each other, just as God in Christ also has forgiven you.

EPHESIANS 4:32 NASB

From time to time, all of us fall prey to a powerful yet subtle temptation: the temptation to judge others. But the Bible teaches us to refrain from such behavior. The warning is unmistakably clear: "Judge not, and ye shall not be judged." In other words, we must refrain from being judgmental . . . or else.

Thankfully, the Bible promises that God has forgiven us (whew!). Now it's our turn to forgive others. So, let us refrain from the temptation to judging our family members, our friends, and our loved ones. And let us refrain from judging people we don't know very well (or people we don't know at all). Instead, let us forgive everybody (including ourselves!) in the same way that God forgives: completely.

We will never comprehend what it cost our Lord in physical agony to offer His forgiveness to everyone—no exceptions.

ANNE GRAHAM LOTZ

The Rock

The Lord is my rock, my fortress, and my deliverer.
PSALM 18:2 HCSB

God is the Creator of life, the Sustainer of life, and the Rock upon which righteous lives are built. God is a never-ending source of support for those who trust Him, and He is a never-ending source of wisdom for those who study His Holy Word.

Is God the Rock upon which you've constructed your own life? If so, then you have chosen wisely. Your faith will give you the inner strength you need to rise above the inevitable demands and struggles of life-here-on-earth.

God will hold your hand and walk with you today and every day if you let Him. Even if your circumstances are difficult, trust the Father. His promises remain true; His love is eternal; and His goodness endures. And because He is the One who can never be moved, you can stand firm in the knowledge that you are protected by Him now and forever.

Accepting His Love

*Praise the Lord, all nations! Glorify Him, all peoples!
For great is His faithful love to us; the Lord's faithfulness
endures forever. Hallelujah!*

PSALM 117 HCSB

The words of 1 John 4:8 teach us that "He who does not love does not know God, for God is love" (NKJV). And because we can be assured that God is love, we can also be assured that God's heart is a loving heart.

God loves you. He loves you more than you can imagine; His affection is deeper than you can fathom. God made you in His own image and gave you salvation through the person of His Son Jesus Christ. And as a result, you have an important decision to make. You must decide what to do about God's love: you can return it . . . or not.

When you accept the love that flows from the heart of God, you are transformed. When you embrace God's love, you feel differently about yourself, your neighbors, your community, your church, and your world. When you open your heart to God's love, you will feel compelled to share God's message—and His compassion—with others.

His Love and Protection

The Lord your God in your midst, The Mighty One, will save; He will rejoice over you with gladness, He will quiet you with His love, He will rejoice over you with singing.

ZEPHANIAH 3:17 NKJV

The hand of God encircles us and comforts us in times of adversity. In times of hardship, He restores our strength; in times of sorrow, He dries our tears. When we are troubled, or weak, or embittered, God is as near as our next breath.

God has promised to protect us, and He intends to fulfill His promise. In a world filled with dangers and temptations, God is the ultimate armor. In a world filled with misleading messages, God's Word is the ultimate truth. In a world filled with more frustrations than we can count, God's Son offers the ultimate peace.

Will you accept God's peace and wear His armor against the dangers of our world? Hopefully so, because when you do, you can live courageously, knowing that you possess the ultimate protection: God's unfailing love for you.

Thank You, Lord, that we may know that our need is never greater than the Helper.

CORRIE TEN BOOM

Hope Now

Without wavering, let us hold tightly to the hope we say we have, for God can be trusted to keep his promise.

HEBREWS 10:23 NLT

Despite God's promises, despite Christ's love, and despite our countless blessings, we frail human beings can still lose hope from time to time. When we do, we need the encouragement of Christian friends, the life-changing power of prayer, and the healing truth of God's Holy Word.

If you find yourself falling into the spiritual traps of worry and discouragement, seek the healing touch of Jesus and the encouraging words of fellow Christians. And remember the words of our Savior: "These things I have spoken unto you, that in me ye might have peace. In the world ye shall have tribulation: but be of good cheer; I have overcome the world" (John 16:33 KJV). This world can be a place of trials and tribulations, but as believers, we are secure. God has promised us peace, joy, and eternal life. And, of course, God keeps His promises today, tomorrow, and forever.

Life with Christ is an endless hope, without him a hopeless end.

ANONYMOUS

Another Day, Countless Opportunities

Therefore, as we have opportunity, we must work for the good of all, especially for those who belong to the household of faith.

GALATIANS 6:10 HCSB

Each day, as we awaken from sleep and begin the new day, we are confronted with countless opportunities to serve God and to worship Him. When we do, He blesses us. But, if we turn our backs to the Creator, or, if we are simply too busy to acknowledge His greatness, we do ourselves a profound disservice.

As women in a fast-changing world, we face challenges that sometimes leave us feeling overworked, over-committed, and overwhelmed. But God has different plans for us. He intends that we take time each day to slow down long enough to praise Him and glorify His Son. When we do, our spirits are calmed and our lives are enriched, as are the lives of our families and friends.

Each day provides a glorious opportunity to place ourselves in the service of the One who is the Giver of all blessings. May we seek His will, trust His word, and place Him where He belongs: at the center of our lives.

Rebellion Against God

He who despises the word will be destroyed, But he who fears the commandment will be rewarded.

PROVERBS 13:13 NKJV

Since God created Adam and Eve, we human beings have been rebelling against our Creator. Why? Because we are unwilling to trust God's Word, and we are unwilling to follow His commandments. God has given us a guidebook for righteous living called the Holy Bible. It contains thorough instructions which, if followed, lead to fulfillment, righteousness and salvation. But, if we choose to ignore God's commandments, the results are as predictable as they are tragic.

Talking about God is easy; living by His commandments is considerably harder. But, unless we are willing to abide by God's laws, all of our righteous proclamations ring hollow. How can we best proclaim our love for the Lord? By obeying Him. And, for further instructions, read the manual.

The pathway of obedience can sometimes be difficult, but it always leads to a strengthening of our inner woman.

VONETTE BRIGHT

When We Must Wait for God

Wait on the Lord, and He will rescue you.

PROVERBS 20:22 HCSB

Life demands patience . . . and lots of it! We live in an imperfect world inhabited by imperfect people. Sometimes, we inherit troubles from others, and sometimes we create trouble for ourselves. In either case, what's required is patience.

Lamentations 3:25-26 reminds us that, "The Lord is wonderfully good to those who wait for him and seek him. So it is good to wait quietly for salvation from the Lord" (NIV). But, for most of us, waiting quietly for God is difficult. Why? Because we are fallible human beings, sometimes quick to anger and sometimes slow to forgive.

The next time you find your patience tested to the limit, remember that the world unfolds according to God's timetable, not ours. Sometimes, we must wait patiently, and that's as it should be. After all, think how patient God has been with us.

Wisdom always waits for the right time to act, while emotion always pushes for action right now.

JOYCE MEYER

The Best Time to Praise Him

But as for me, I will always have hope; I will praise you more and more.

PSALM 71:14 NIV

When is the best time to praise God? In church? Before dinner is served? When we tuck little children into bed? None of the above. The best time to praise God is all day, every day, to the greatest extent we can, with thanksgiving in our hearts.

Too many of us, even well-intentioned believers, tend to "compartmentalize" our waking hours into a few familiar categories: work, rest, play, family time, and worship. To do so is a mistake. Worship and praise should be woven into the fabric of everything we do; it should never be relegated to a weekly three-hour visit to church on Sunday morning.

Mrs. Charles E. Cowman, the author of the classic devotional text Streams in the Desert, wrote, "Two wings are necessary to lift our souls toward God: prayer and praise. Prayer asks. Praise accepts the answer." Today, find a little more time to lift your concerns to God in prayer, and praise Him for all that He has done. He's listening . . . and He wants to hear from you.

He Deserves Your Best

For each tree is known by its own fruit.

LUKE 6:44 HCSB

God deserves your best. Is He getting it? Do you make an appointment with your Heavenly Father each day? Do you carve out moments when He receives your undivided attention? Or is your devotion to Him fleeting, distracted, and sporadic?

When you acquire the habit of focusing your heart and mind squarely upon God's intentions for your life, He will guide your steps and bless your endeavors. But if you allow distractions to take priority over your relationship with God, they will—and you will pay a price for your mistaken priorities.

Today, focus upon God's Word and upon His will for your life. When you do, you'll be amazed at how quickly everything else comes into focus, too.

Jesus challenges you and me to keep our focus daily on the cross of His will if we want to be His disciples.

ANNE GRAHAM LOTZ

The Merry-Go-Round

I will give you a new heart and put a new spirit within you.

Ezekiel 36:26 HCSB

For busy women living in a fast-paced 21st century world, life may seem like a merry-go-round that never stops turning. If that description seems to fit your life, then you may find yourself running short of patience, or strength, or both.

When you feel tired or discouraged, there is a source from which you can draw the power needed to recharge your spiritual batteries. That source is God.

Are you exhausted or troubled? Weak or worried? Worn out or burned out? If so, take time to rest, and take time to have a heart-to-heart talk with God. When you do, you'll discover that the Creator of the universe can help you gain a renewed sense of hope and a fresh perspective . . . your job is to let Him do it.

Jesus, my Savior, look on me, for I am weary and oppressed; I come to cast myself on Thee: Thou art my Rest.

Charlotte Elliott

Seeking God

You will seek me and find me when you seek me with all your heart.

JEREMIAH 29:13 NIV

The familiar words of Matthew 6 remind us that, as believers, we must seek God and His kingdom. And when we seek Him with our hearts open and our prayers lifted, we need not look far: God is with us always.

Sometimes, however, in the crush of our daily duties, God may seem far away, but He is not. God is everywhere we have ever been and everywhere we will ever go. He is with us night and day; He knows our thoughts and our prayers. And, when we earnestly seek Him, we will find Him because He is here, waiting patiently for us to reach out to Him.

Today, let us reach out to the Giver of all blessings. Let us turn to Him for guidance and for strength. Today, may we, who have been given so much, seek God and invite Him into every aspect of our lives. And, let us remember that no matter our circumstances, God never leaves us; He is here . . . always right here.

One must see God in everyone.

CATHERINE LABOURE

He Wants Your Attention

Let us lay aside every weight and the sin that so easily ensnares us, and run with endurance the race that lies before us, keeping our eyes on Jesus, the source and perfecter of our faith.

HEBREWS 12:1-2 HCSB

Is yours a life of moderation or accumulation? Are you more interested in the possessions you can acquire or in the person you can become? The answers to these questions will determine the direction of your day and, in time, the direction of your life.

Ours is a highly complicated society, a place where people and corporations vie for your attention, for your time, and for your dollars. Don't let them succeed in complicating your life! Keep your eyes focused instead upon God.

If your material possessions are somehow distancing you from God, discard them. If your outside interests leave you too little time for your family or your Creator, slow down the merry-go-round, or better yet, get off the merry-go-round completely. Remember: God wants your full attention, and He wants it today, so don't let anybody or anything get in His way.

Sharing Your Testimony

And I say to you, anyone who acknowledges Me before men, the Son of Man will also acknowledge him before the angels of God.

Luke 12:8 HCSB

Our personal testimonies are extremely important, but sometimes, because of shyness or insecurities, we're afraid to share our experiences. And that's unfortunate.

In his second letter to Timothy, Paul shares a message to believers of every generation when he writes, "God has not given us a spirit of timidity" (1:7). Paul's meaning is clear: When sharing our beliefs, we, as Christians, must be courageous, forthright, and unashamed.

We live in a world that desperately needs the healing message of Christ Jesus. Every believer, each in his or her own way, bears responsibility for sharing the Good News of our Savior.

Billy Graham observed, "Our faith grows by expression. If we want to keep our faith, we must share it." If you are a follower of Christ, the time to express your belief in Him is now. You know how He has touched your heart; help Him do the same for others.

He Changes You

I'm baptizing you here in the river, turning your old life in for a kingdom life. His baptism—a holy baptism by the Holy Spirit—will change you from the inside out.

MARK 1:8 MSG

God has the power to transform your life if you invite Him to do so. Your decision is straightforward: whether or not to allow the Father's transforming power to work in you and through you. God stands at the door and waits; all you must do is knock. When you do, God always answers.

Are you in need of a new beginning? If so, turn your heart toward God in prayer. Are you weak or worried? Take the time—or, more accurately, make the time—to delve deeply into God's Holy Word. Are you spiritually depleted? Call upon fellow believers to support you, and call upon Christ to renew your sense of joy and thanksgiving. When you do, you'll discover that the Creator of the universe is in the business of making all things new—including you.

For God is, indeed, a wonderful Father who longs to pour out His mercy upon us, and whose majesty is so great that He can transform us from deep within.

ST. TERESA OF AVILA

Touched by the Savior

And when the woman saw that she was not hid, she came trembling, and falling down before him, she declared unto him before all the people for what cause she had touched him, and how she was healed immediately. And he said unto her, Daughter, be of good comfort: thy faith hath made thee whole; go in peace.

LUKE 8:47-48 KJV

Until we have been touched by the Savior, we can never be completely whole. Until we have placed our hearts and our lives firmly in the hands of the living Christ, we are incomplete. Until we come to know Jesus, we long for a sense of peace that continues to elude us no matter how diligently we search.

It is only through God that we discover genuine peace. We can search far and wide for worldly substitutes, but when we seek peace apart from God, we will find neither peace nor God.

As believers, we are invited to accept the "peace that passes all understanding" (Philippians 4:7 NIV). That peace, of course, is God's peace. Let us accept His peace, and let us share it today, tomorrow, and every day that we live.

Taking Your Worries to God

Give your worries to the Lord, and he will take care of you.
He will never let good people down.

PSALM 55:22 NCV

Because life is sometimes difficult, and because we have understandable fears about the uncertainty of the future, we worry. At times, we may find ourselves fretting over the countless details of everyday life. We may worry about our relationships, our finances, our health, or any number of potential problems, some large and some small.

If you're a "worrier" by nature, it's probably time to rethink the way that you think! Perhaps you've formed the unfortunate habit of focusing too intently on negative aspects of life while spending too little time counting your blessings. If so, take your worries to God . . . and leave them there. When you do, you'll learn to worry a little less and to trust God a little more—and that's as it should be because God is trustworthy, you are protected, and your future can be intensely bright.

If you can't sleep, don't count sheep; talk to the Shepherd.

ANONYMOUS

Our Hopes and His Peace

And as they thus spake, Jesus himself stood in the midst of them, and saith unto them, Peace be unto you.

LUKE 24:36 KJV

The beautiful words of John 14:27 give us hope: "Peace I leave with you, my peace I give unto you . . . ." Jesus offers us peace, not as the world gives, but as He alone gives. We, as believers, can accept His peace or ignore it.

When we accept the peace of Jesus Christ into our hearts, our lives are transformed. And then, because we possess the gift of peace, we can share that gift with fellow Christians, family members, friends, and associates. If, on the other hand, we choose to ignore the gift of peace—for whatever reason—we cannot share what we do not possess.

As every woman knows, peace can be a scarce commodity in a demanding, 21st-Century world. How, then, can we find the peace that we so desperately desire? By turning our days and our lives over to God. May we give our lives, our hopes, and our prayers to the Lord, and, by doing so, accept His will and His peace.

The Wisdom to Be Humble

Do you want to be counted wise, to build a reputation for wisdom? Here's what you do: Live well, live wisely, live humbly.

JAMES 3:13 MSG

Humility is not, in most cases, a naturally occurring human trait. Most of us, it seems, are more than willing to overestimate our own accomplishments. We are tempted to say, "Look how wonderful I am!" . . . hoping all the while that the world will agree with our own self-appraisals. But those of us who fall prey to the sin of pride should beware—God is definitely not impressed by our prideful proclamations.

God honors humility . . . and He rewards those who humbly serve Him. So if you've acquired the wisdom to be humble, then you are to be congratulated. But if you've not yet overcome the tendency to overestimate your own accomplishments, then God still has some important (and perhaps painful) lessons to teach you— lessons about humility that you still need to learn.

We are never stronger than the moment we admit we are weak.

BETH MOORE

Accepting His Abundance

*Live in me. Make your home in me just as I do in you.
In the same way that a branch can't bear grapes by itself
but only by being joined to the vine, you can't bear fruit
unless you are joined with me. I am the Vine, you are the
branches. When you're joined with me and I with you,
the relation intimate and organic, the harvest is sure to
be abundant.*

JOHN 15:4-5 MSG

A re you the kind of woman who accepts God's
spiritual abundance without reservation? If so,
you are availing yourself of the peace and the joy that
He has promised. Do you sincerely seek the riches that
our Savior offers to those who give themselves to Him?
Then follow Him. When you do, you will receive the
love and the abundance that Jesus offers to those who
follow Him.

Seek first the salvation that is available through a
personal, passionate relationship with Christ, and then
claim the joy, the peace, and the spiritual abundance
that the Shepherd offers His sheep.

About Anger

When you are angry, do not sin, and be sure to stop being angry before the end of the day. Do not give the devil a way to defeat you.

EPHESIANS 4:26-27 NCV

Sometimes, anger is appropriate. Even Jesus became angry when confronted with the moneychangers in the temple. On occasion, you, like Jesus, will confront evil, and when you do, you may respond as He did: vigorously and without reservation. But, more often than not, your frustrations will be of the more mundane variety. As long as you live here on earth, you will face countless opportunities to lose your temper over small, relatively insignificant events: a traffic jam, a spilled cup of coffee, an inconsiderate comment, a broken promise. When you are tempted to lose your temper over the minor inconveniences of life, don't. Turn away from anger, hatred, bitterness, and regret. Turn instead to God.

Life is too short to spend it being angry, bored, or dull.

BARBARA JOHNSON

Your Beliefs and Your Life

For the kingdom of God is not in talk but in power.

1 CORINTHIANS 4:20 HCSB

Do you weave your beliefs into the very fabric of your day. If you do, God will honor your good works, and your good works will honor God.

If you seek to be a responsible believer, you must realize that it is never enough to hear the instructions of God; you must also live by them. And it is never enough to wait idly by while others do God's work here on earth. You, too, must act.

Doing God's work is a responsibility that every Christian (including you) should bear. And when you do, your loving Heavenly Father will reward your efforts with a bountiful harvest.

God delights to meet the faith of one who looks up to Him and says, "Lord, You know that I cannot do this— but I believe that You can!"

AMY CARMICHAEL

He Does Not Change

One Lord, one faith, one baptism, one God and Father of all, who is above all and through all and in all.

EPHESIANS 4:5-6 HCSB

We live in a world that is always changing, but we worship a God that never changes—thank goodness! As believers, we can be comforted in the knowledge that our Heavenly Father is the rock that simply cannot be moved: "I am the Lord, I do not change" (Malachi 3:6 NKJV).

Are you facing difficult circumstances or unwelcome changes? If so, please remember that God is far bigger than any problem you may face. So, instead of worrying about life's inevitable challenges, put your faith in the Father and His only begotten Son: "Jesus Christ is the same yesterday, today, and forever" (Hebrews 13:8 HCSB). And rest assured: It is precisely because your Savior does not change that you can face your challenges with courage for this day and hope for the future.

Let nothing disturb you, nothing frighten you; all things are passing; God never changes.

ST. TERESA OF AVILA

Claiming Contentment in a Discontented World

But godliness with contentment is a great gain.

1 Timothy 6:6 HCSB

Everywhere we turn, or so it seems, the world promises us contentment and happiness. We are bombarded by messages offering us the "good life" if only we will purchase products and services that are designed to provide happiness, success, and contentment. But the contentment that the world offers is fleeting and incomplete. Thankfully, the contentment that God offers is all encompassing and everlasting.

Happiness depends less upon our circumstances than upon our thoughts. When we turn our thoughts to God, to His gifts, and to His glorious creation, we experience the joy that God intends for His children. But, when we focus on the negative aspects of life—or when we disobey God's commandments—we cause ourselves needless suffering.

Do you sincerely want to be a contented Christian? Then set your mind and your heart upon God's love and His grace. Seek first the salvation that is available through a personal relationship with Jesus Christ, and then claim the joy, the contentment, and the spiritual abundance that God offers His children.

When the Seas Aren't Calm

*He replied, "You of little faith, why are you so afraid?"
Then he got up and rebuked the winds and the waves, and
it was completely calm.*

MATTHEW 8:26 NIV

Sometimes the seas of life are calm, and sometimes they are not. When we find ourselves beset by the inevitable storms of life, we may sense that all is lost—but if we imagine, even for a moment, that all hope is gone, we are mistaken.

The Bible is unambiguous: it promises that God will remain steadfast, even during our darkest hours. God's Word makes it clear that He is with us always, on good days and bad days. He never leaves our side, and He never stops loving us.

So if you're feeling buffeted by the winds and the waves of life, don't despair. God is not just near, He is here. He has promised to protect you now and forever. And upon that promise, you can always depend.

When life is difficult, God wants us to have a faith that trusts and waits.

KAY ARTHUR

The Power of Encouragement

*He comes alongside us when we go through hard times,
and before you know it, he brings us alongside someone
else who is going through hard times so that we can be
there for that person just as God was there for us.*

2 CORINTHIANS 1:4 MSG

Do you delight in the victories of others? You should. Each day provides countless opportunities to encourage others and to praise their good works. When you do so, you spread seeds of joy and happiness.

American poet Ella Wheeler Wilcox advised, "Talk happiness. The world is sad enough without your woe." Her words still apply.

Life is a team sport, and all of us need occasional pats on the back from our teammates. So, let us be cheerful with smiles on our faces and encouraging words on our lips. By blessing others, we also bless ourselves, and, when we do, God smiles.

The overall goal in helping any individual is to communicate hope, that they might more courageously and confidently face daily life with its trials and struggles.

VERNA BIRKEY

Living in a Fear-based World

I sought the LORD, and he answered me; he delivered me from all my fears.

PSALM 34:4 NIV

We live in a fear-based world, a world where bad new travels at light speed and good news doesn't. These are troubled times, times when we have legitimate fears for the future of our nation, our world, and our families. But as Christians, we have every reason to live courageously. After all, the ultimate battle has already been fought and won on that faraway cross at Calvary.

Perhaps you, like countless other believers, have found your courage tested by the anxieties and fears that are an inevitable part of 21st-Century life. If so, God wants to have a little chat with you. The next time you find your courage tested to the limit, God wants to remind you that He is not just near, He is here.

Your Heavenly Father is your Protector and your Deliverer. Call upon Him in your hour of need, and be comforted. Whatever your challenge, whatever your trouble, God can handle it. And will.

He Taught Us to Be Generous

I have shown you in every way, by laboring like this, that you must support the weak. And remember the words of the Lord Jesus, that He said, "It is more blessed to give than to receive."

Acts 20:35 NKJV

The thread of generosity is woven—completely and inextricably—into the very fabric of Christ's teachings. As He sent His disciples out to heal the sick and spread God's message of salvation, Jesus offered this guiding principle: Freely you have received, freely give. (Matthew 10:8 NIV) The principle still applies. If we are to be disciples of Christ, we must give freely of our time, our possessions, and our love.

Lisa Whelchel spoke for Christian women everywhere when she observed, "The Lord has abundantly blessed me all of my life. I'm not trying to pay Him back for all of His wonderful gifts; I just realize that He gave them to me to give away." All of us have been blessed, and all of us are called to share those blessings without reservation.

Today, make this pledge and keep it: Be a cheerful, generous, courageous giver. The world needs your help, and you need the spiritual rewards that will be yours when you share your possessions, your talents, and your time.

God's Eternal Presence

And the world with its lust is passing away, but the one who does God's will remains forever.

1 JOHN 2:17 HCSB

God's hand is ever-present and everlasting. It has created the universe—and everything in it—out of nothingness. God's hand is everywhere you have ever been, and it is everywhere you will ever be. Your obligation, as a believer, is to reach out to Him and accept the peace, the love, the abundance, and the grace that He has offered.

Are you tired? Discouraged? Fearful? Be comforted. God's hand is with you. Are you worried or anxious? Be confident in God's power. He will never desert you. Are you grieving? Know that God understands your suffering. And rest assured that He will comfort you and that, in time, He will dry your tears.

Throughout every season of life, in times of celebration or sorrow, in times of victory or defeat, God's hand is not just near; it is always here. So why not reach out to Him right now?

He is more within us than we are ourselves.

ELIZABETH ANN SETON

He Has a Plan for You

You will show me the path of life; in Your presence is fullness of joy; at Your right hand are pleasures forevermore.

PSALM 16:11 NKJV

God has a plan for your life. He understands that plan as thoroughly and completely as He knows you. And, if you seek God's will earnestly and prayerfully, He will make His plans known to you in His own time and in His own way.

If you sincerely seek to live in accordance with God's will for your life, you will live in accordance with His commandments. You will study God's Word, and you will be watchful for His signs.

Sometimes, God's plans seem unmistakably clear to you. But other times, He may lead you through the wilderness before He directs you to the Promised Land. So be patient and keep seeking His will for your life. When you do, you'll be amazed at the marvelous things that an all-powerful, all-knowing God can do.

God will never lead you where His strength cannot keep you.

BARBARA JOHNSON

Seeking His Will

Teach me to do Your will, for You are my God; Your Spirit is good. Lead me in the land of uprightness.

PSALM 143:10 NKJV

The Book of Judges (chapters 4 and 5) tells the story of Deborah, the fearless woman who helped lead the army of Israel to victory over the Canaanites. Deborah was a judge and a prophetess, a woman called by God to lead her people. And when she answered God's call, she was rewarded with one of the great victories of Old Testament times.

Like Deborah, all of us are called to serve our Creator. And, like Deborah, we may sometimes find ourselves facing trials that can bring trembling to the very depths of our souls. As believers, we must seek God's will and follow it. When we do, we are reward with victories, some great and some small.

As this day unfolds, seek God's will for your own life and obey His Word. When you entrust your life to Him completely and without reservation, He will give you the strength to meet any challenge, the courage to face any trial, and the wisdom to live in His righteousness and in His peace.

Happiness Now

For the happy heart, life is a continual feast.

PROVERBS 15:15 NLT

Happiness depends less upon our circumstances than upon our thoughts. When we turn our thoughts to God, to His gifts, and to His glorious creation, we experience the joy that God intends for His children. But, when we focus on the negative aspects of life, we suffer needlessly.

Do you sincerely want to be a happy Christian? Then set your mind and your heart upon God's love and His grace. The fullness of life in Christ is available to all who seek it and claim it. Count yourself among that number. Seek first the salvation that is available through a personal relationship with Jesus Christ, and then claim the joy, the peace, and the spiritual abundance that the Shepherd offers His sheep.

Smile—it increases your face value.

ANONYMOUS

Those who are God's without reserve are, in every sense, content.

HANNAH WHITALL SMITH

Judge Not

You, therefore, have no excuse, you who pass judgment on someone else, for at whatever point you judge the other, you are condemning yourself.

ROMANS 2:1 NIV

The warning of Matthew 7:1 is clear: "Judge not, that ye be not judged" (KJV). Yet even the most devoted Christians may fall prey to a powerful yet subtle temptation: the temptation to judge others. But as obedient followers of Christ, we are commanded to refrain from such behavior.

As Jesus came upon a young woman who had been condemned by the Pharisees, He spoke not only to the crowd that was gathered there, but also to all generations when He warned, "He that is without sin among you, let him first cast a stone at her" (John 8:7 KJV). Christ's message is clear, and it applies not only to the Pharisees of ancient times, but also to us.

Only Christ can free us from the prison of legalism, and then only if we are willing to be freed.

MADELEINE L'ENGLE

He Is at Work

*You are the God who works wonders; You revealed Your
strength among the peoples.*

PSALM 77:14 HCSB

Do you believe that God is at work in the world?
And do you also believe that nothing is impossible
for Him? If so, then you also believe that God is perfectly
capable of doing things that you, as a mere human being
with limited vision and limited understanding, would
deem to be utterly impossible. And that's precisely what
God does.

Since the moment that He created our universe out of
nothingness, God has made a habit of doing miraculous
things. And He still works miracles today. Expect Him
to work miracles in your own life, and then be watchful.
With God, absolutely nothing is impossible, including
an amazing assortment of miracles that He stands ready,
willing, and able to perform for you and yours.

Are you looking for a miracle? If you keep your eyes
wide open and trust in God, you won't have to look
very far.

MARIE T. FREEMAN

Making Peace with the Past

Do not remember the past events, pay no attention to things of old. Look, I am about to do something new; even now it is coming. Do you not see it? Indeed, I will make a way in the wilderness, rivers in the desert.

ISAIAH 43:18-19 HCSB

Have you made peace with your past? If so, congratulations. But, if you are mired in the quicksand of regret, it's time to plan your escape. How can you do so? By accepting what has been and by trusting God for what will be.

Because you are human, you may be slow to forget yesterday's disappointments; if so you are not alone. But if you sincerely seek to focus your hopes and energies on the future, then you must find ways to accept the past, no matter how difficult it may be to do so.

If you have not yet made peace with the past, today is the day to declare an end to all hostilities. When you do, you can then turn your thoughts to wondrous promises of God and to the glorious future that He has in store for you.

The cross takes care of the past. The cross takes care of the flesh. The cross takes care of the world.

KAY ARTHUR

Making God's Priorities Your Priorities

Lord, teach me your demands, and I will keep them until the end.

PSALM 119:33 NCV

Sometimes, amid the demands of daily life, we lose perspective. Life seems out of balance, and the pressures of everyday living seem overwhelming. What's needed is a fresh perspective, a restored sense of balance . . . and God.

If a temporary loss of perspective has left you worried, exhausted, or both, it's time to readjust your thought patterns. Negative thoughts are habit-forming; thankfully, so are positive ones. With practice, you can form the habit of focusing on God's priorities and your possibilities. When you do, you'll soon discover that you will spend less time fretting about your challenges and more time praising God for His gifts.

When you call upon the Lord and prayerfully seek His will, He will give you wisdom and perspective. When you make God's priorities your priorities, He will direct your steps and calm your fears. So today and every day hereafter, pray for a sense of balance and perspective. And remember: your thoughts are intensely powerful things, so handle them with care.

Whose Expectations?

The person who knows my commandments and keeps them, that's who loves me. And the person who loves me will be loved by my Father, and I will love him and make myself plain to him.

JOHN 14:21 MSG

Here's a quick quiz: Whose expectations are you trying to meet?

A. Your friends' expectations B. Society's expectations C. God's expectations

If you're a Christian, the correct answer is C., but if you're overly concerned with either A. or B., you're not alone. Plenty of people invest too much energy trying to meet society's expectations and too little energy trying to please God. It's a common behavior, but it's also a very big mistake.

A better strategy, of course, is to try to please God first. To do so, you must prioritize your day according to God's commandments, and you must seek His will and His wisdom in all matters.

Are you having trouble choosing between God's priorities and society's priorities? If so, turn the concerns over to God—prayerfully, earnestly, and often. Then, listen for His answer . . . and trust the answer He gives.

The World Needs Your Prayer

Then if my people who are called by my name will humble themselves and pray and seek my face and turn from their wicked ways, I will hear from heaven and will forgive their sins and heal their land.

2 CHRONICLES 7:14 NLT

This troubled world desperately needs your prayers, and so does your family. When you weave the habit of prayer into the very fabric of your day, you invite God to become a partner in every aspect of your life. When you consult God on an hourly basis, you avail yourself of His wisdom, His strength, and His love. And, because God answers prayers according to His perfect timetable, your petitions to Him will transform your family, your world, and yourself.

Today, turn everything over to your Creator in prayer. Instead of worrying about your next decision, decide to let God lead the way. Don't limit your prayers to meals or to bedtime. Pray constantly about things great and small. God is listening, and He wants to hear from you. Now.

God answers prayers—not advice.

ANONYMOUS

At Peace with Your Purpose

The Lord will work out his plans for my life—for your
faithful love, O Lord, endures forever.

PSALM 138:8 NLT

Are you at peace with the direction of your life? If you're a Christian, you should be. Even if God's plans for you are uncertain, His love for you is not.

The familiar words of John 14:27 give us hope: "Peace I leave with you, My peace I give unto you . . . ." Jesus offers us peace, not as the world gives, but as He alone gives. We, as believers, can accept His peace or ignore it.

When we accept the peace of Jesus Christ into our hearts, our lives are transformed. And then, because we possess the gift of peace, we can share that gift with fellow believers, family members, friends, and associates.

Today, as a gift to yourself, to your family, and to your friends, claim the inner peace that is your spiritual birthright: the peace of Jesus Christ. It is offered freely; it has been paid for in full; it is yours for the asking. So ask. And then share.

The first step to becoming is to will it.

MOTHER TERESA

A Righteous Life

But seek first the kingdom of God and His righteousness, and all these things shall be added to you.

MATTHEW 6:33 NKJV

A righteous life has many components: faith, honesty, generosity, love, kindness, humility, gratitude, and worship, to name but a few. If we seek to follow the steps of our Savior, Jesus Christ, we must seek to live according to His commandments. In short, we must, to the best of our abilities, live according to the principles contained in God's Holy Word.

The Holy Bible contains thorough instructions which, if followed, lead to fulfillment, righteousness, and salvation. But, if we choose to ignore God's commandments, the results are as predictable as they are tragic. Let us follow God's commandments, and let us conduct our lives in such a way that we might be shining examples for those who have not yet found Christ.

Holiness is not just a job description for ministers, but it is a command for all who assemble before the holy God.

LISA BEVERE

The Power of Silence

Truly my soul silently waits for God; from Him comes my salvation.

PSALM 62:1 NKJV

Do you take time each day for an extended period of silence? And during those precious moments, do you sincerely open your heart to your Creator? If so, you are wise and you are blessed.

The world can be a noisy place, a place filled to the brim with distractions, interruptions, and frustrations. And if you're not careful, the struggles and stresses of everyday living can rob you of the peace that should rightfully be yours because of your personal relationship with Christ. So take time each day to quietly commune with your Savior. When you do, those moments of silence will enable you to participate more fully in the only source of peace that endures: God's peace.

If you, too, will learn to wait upon God, to get alone with Him, and remain silent so that you can hear His voice when He is ready to speak to you, what a difference it will make in you life!

KAY ARTHUR

Rebels Beware

Whoever is stubborn after being corrected many times will suddenly be hurt beyond cure.

PROVERBS 29:1 NCV

Since the days of Adam and Eve, human beings have been strong-willed and rebellious. Our rebellion stems, in large part, from an intense desire to do things "our way" instead of "God's way." But when we pridefully choose to forsake God's path for our lives, we do ourselves a sincere injustice . . . and we are penalized because of our stubbornness.

God's Word warns us to be humble, not prideful. God instructs us to be obedient, not rebellious. God wants us to do things His way. When we do, we reap a bountiful harvest of blessings—more blessings than we can count. But when we pridefully rebel against our Creator, we sow the seeds of our own destruction, and we reap a sad, sparse, bitter harvest. May we sow—and reap—accordingly.

God loves us enough to make us ultimately miserable in our rebellion.

BETH MOORE

The Gift of Time

Hard work means prosperity; only fools idle away their time.

PROVERBS 12:11 NLT

Time is a nonrenewable gift from God. But sometimes, we treat our time here on earth as if it were not a gift at all: We may be tempted to invest our lives in trivial pursuits and petty diversions. But our Father beckons each of us to a higher calling.

An important element of our stewardship to God is the way that we choose to spend the time He has entrusted to us. Each waking moment holds the potential to do a good deed, to say a kind word, or to offer a heartfelt prayer. Our challenge, as believers, is use our time wisely in the service of God's work and in accordance with His plan for our lives.

Each day is a special treasure to be savored and celebrated. May we—as Christians who have so much to celebrate—never fail to praise our Creator by rejoicing in His glorious creation and by using it wisely.

Faith Tip:
If you don't value your time . . .
neither will anybody else.

Serenity

Those who love your law have great peace and do not stumble.

PSALM 119:165 NLT

When you encounter unfortunate circumstances that are beyond your power to control, here's a proven way to retain your sanity: accept those circumstances (no matter how unpleasant), and trust God.

The American Theologian Reinhold Niebuhr composed a profoundly simple verse that came to be known as the Serenity Prayer: "God, grant me the serenity to accept the things I cannot change, the courage to change the things I can, and the wisdom to know the difference." Niebuhr's words are far easier to recite than they are to live by. Why? Because most of us want life to unfold in accordance with our own wishes and timetables. But sometimes God has other plans.

When you trust God, you can be comforted in the knowledge that your Creator is both loving and wise, and that He understands His plans perfectly, even when you do not.

What's Your Attitude?

Set your minds on what is above, not on what is on the earth.

COLOSSIANS 3:2 HCSB

What's your attitude today? Are you fearful, angry, bored, or worried? Are you worried more about pleasing your friends than about pleasing your God? Are you confused, bitter or pessimistic? If so, God wants to have a little talk with you.

God created you in His own image, and He wants you to experience joy and abundance. But, God will not force His joy upon you; you must claim it for yourself. So today, and every day thereafter, celebrate this life that God has given you. Think optimistically about yourself and your future. Give thanks to the One who has given you everything, and trust in your heart that He wants to give you so much more.

Some people complain that God put thorns on roses, while others praise Him for putting roses on thorns.

ANONYMOUS

The greater part of our happiness or misery depends on our dispositions, and not on our circumstances.

MARTHA WASHINGTON

Too Busy

Don't burn out; keep yourselves fueled and aflame. Be alert servants of the Master, cheerfully expectant. Don't quit in hard times; pray all the harder.

ROMANS 12:11-12 MSG

Has the busy pace of life robbed you of the peace that might otherwise be yours through Jesus Christ? If so, you are simply too busy for your own good. Through His Son Jesus, God offers you a peace that passes human understanding, but He won't force His peace upon you; in order to experience it, you must slow down long enough to sense His presence and His love.

Today, as a gift to yourself, to your family, and to the world, slow down and claim the inner peace that is your spiritual birthright: the peace of Jesus Christ. It is offered freely; it has been paid for in full; it is yours for the asking. So ask. And then share.

Frustration is not the will of God. There is time to do anything and everything that God wants us to do.

ELISABETH ELLIOT

Choices, Choices, Choices

Don't depend on your own wisdom. Respect the Lord and refuse to do wrong.

PROVERBS 3:7 NCV

Life is a series of choices. Each day, we make countless decisions that can bring us closer to God...or not. When we obey God, we are blessed. But, when we turn our backs upon Him by disobeying His commandments, we must suffer the consequences.

Do you seek spiritual abundance that can be yours through the person of God's only begotten Son? Then invite Christ into your heart and live according to His teachings. And, when you confront a difficult decision or a powerful temptation, seek God's wisdom and trust it. When you do, you will receive untold blessings—not only for this day, but also for all eternity.

Choices can change our lives profoundly. The choice to mend a broken relationship, to say "yes" to a difficult assignment, to lay aside some important work to play with a child, to visit some forgotten person—these small choices may affect many lives eternally.

GLORIA GAITHER

Considering the Cross

Christ did not send me to baptize people but to preach the Good News. And he sent me to preach the Good News without using words of human wisdom so that the cross of Christ would not lose its power.

1 CORINTHIANS 1:17 NCV

As we consider Christ's sacrifice on the cross, we should be profoundly humbled and profoundly grateful. And today, as we come to Christ in prayer, we should do so in a spirit of quiet, heartfelt devotion to the One who gave His life so that we might have life eternal.

He was the Son of God, but He wore a crown of thorns. He was the Savior of mankind, yet He was put to death on a roughhewn cross made of wood. He offered His healing touch to an unsaved world, and yet the same hands that had healed the sick and raised the dead were pierced with nails.

Christ humbled Himself on a cross—for you. He shed His blood—for you. He has offered to walk with you through this life and throughout all eternity. As you approach Him today in prayer, think about His sacrifice and His grace. And be humble.

The Importance of Discipline

For God has not given us a spirit of fear and timidity, but of power, love, and self-discipline. So you must never be ashamed to tell others about our Lord.

2 TIMOTHY 1:7-8 NLT

Wise women understand the importance of discipline. In Proverbs 28:19, the message is clear: "Those who work their land will have plenty of food, but the ones who chase empty dreams instead will end up poor" (NCV).

If we work diligently and faithfully, we can expect a bountiful harvest. But we must never expect the harvest to precede the labor.

Poet Mary Frances Butts advised, "Build a little fence of trust around today. Fill each space with loving work, and therein stay." And her words still apply.

Thoughtful women understand that God doesn't reward laziness or misbehavior. To the contrary, God expects His children (of all ages) to lead disciplined lives . . . and when they do, He rewards them.

The goal of any discipline is to result in greater freedom. Gal. 5:1

ANONYMOUS

Beyond Our Obstacles

Even though good people may be bothered by trouble seven times, they are never defeated.

PROVERBS 24:16 NCV

The occasional disappointments and failures of life are inevitable. Such setbacks are simply the price that we must occasionally pay for our willingness to take risks as we follow our dreams. But even when we encounter bitter disappointments, we must never lose faith.

The reassuring words of Hebrews 10:36 remind us that when we persevere, we will eventually receive that which God has promised. What's required is perseverance, not perfection.

When we encounter the inevitable difficulties of daily life, God stands ready to protect us. Our responsibility, of course, is to ask Him for protection. When we call upon Him in heartfelt prayer, He will answer—in His own time and according to His own plan—and He will heal us. And, while we are waiting for God's plans to unfold and for His healing touch to restore us, we can be comforted in the knowledge that our Creator can overcome any obstacle, even if we cannot.

Following Christ

But whoever keeps His word, truly in him the love of God is perfected. This is how we know we are in Him: the one who says he remains in Him should walk just as He walked.

1 JOHN 2:5-6 HCSB

Each day, as we awaken from sleep, we are confronted with countless opportunities to serve God and to follow in the footsteps of His Son. When we do, our Heavenly Father guides our steps and blesses our endeavors.

As citizens of a fast-changing world, we face challenges that sometimes leave us feeling overworked, over-committed, and overwhelmed. But God has different plans for us. He intends that we slow down long enough to praise Him and to glorify His Son. When we do, He lifts our spirits and enriches our lives.

Today provides a glorious opportunity to place yourself in the service of the One who is the Giver of all blessings. May you seek His will, may you trust His word, and may you walk in the footsteps of His Son.

When We Cannot Understand

"For my thoughts are not your thoughts, neither are your ways my ways," declares the LORD. "As the heavens are higher than the earth, so are my ways higher than your ways and my thoughts that your thoughts."

ISAIAH 55:8-9 NIV

Try though we might, we simply cannot understand God. We can see His handiwork; we can feel His presence; we can worship His Son; but as mere mortals, we lack the capacity to comprehend a being of infinite power and infinite love. Someday, we will understand Him completely, but until then, we must trust Him completely.

The journey through life leads us over many peaks and through many valleys. When we reach the mountaintops, we find it easy to praise God, to trust Him, and to give thanks. But, when we trudge through the dark valleys of bitterness and despair, trusting God is more difficult.

When our courage is tested to the limit, we must lean upon God's promises. And we must remember that God rules both mountaintops and valleys—with limitless wisdom and unchanging love—now and forever.

Embracing God's Love

We love him, because he first loved us.

1 JOHN 4:19 KJV

As a woman, you know the profound love that you hold in your heart for your own family and friends. As a child of God, you can only imagine the infinite love that your Heavenly Father holds for you.

God made you in His own image and gave you salvation through the person of His Son Jesus Christ. And now, precisely because you are a wondrous creation treasured by God, a question presents itself: What will you do in response to the Creator's love? Will you ignore it or embrace it?

When you embrace God's love, your life's purpose is forever changed. When you embrace God's love, you feel differently about yourself, your neighbors, your family, and your world. More importantly, you share God's message—and His love—with others.

Your Heavenly Father—a God of infinite love and mercy—is waiting to embrace you with open arms. Accept His love today and forever.

Protected by the Hand of God

For whatever is born of God overcomes the world. And this is the victory that has overcome the world—our faith.

1 JOHN 5:4 NKJV

Have you ever faced challenges that seemed too big to handle? Have you ever faced big problems that, despite your best efforts, simply could not be solved? If so, you know how uncomfortable it is to feel helpless in the face of difficult circumstances. Thankfully, even when there's nowhere else to turn, you can turn your thoughts and prayers to God, and He will respond.

God's hand uplifts those who turn their hearts and prayers to Him. Count yourself among that number. When you do, you can live courageously and joyfully, knowing that "this too will pass"—but that God's love for you will not. And you can draw strength from the knowledge that you are a marvelous creation, loved, protected, and uplifted by the ever-present hand of God.

God will take care of everything—the rest is up to you.

LISA WHELCHEL

DAY 236

He Overcomes the World

God decided to let his people know this rich and glorious secret which he has for all people. This secret is Christ himself, who is in you. He is our only hope for glory.

COLOSSIANS 1:27 NCV

There are few sadder sights on earth than the sight of a person who has lost all hope. In difficult times, hope can be elusive, but Christians need never lose it. After all, God is good; His love endures; He has promised His children the gift of eternal life.

If you find yourself falling into the spiritual traps of worry and discouragement, consider the words of Jesus. It was Christ who promised, "In the world you will have tribulation; but be of good cheer, I have overcome the world." (John 16:33 NKJV). This world is, indeed, a place of trials and tribulations, but as believers, we are secure. God has promised us peace, joy, and eternal life. And, of course, God always keeps His promises.

The only hope we have is the only hope we've ever had.

ANGELA THOMAS

Light of the World

I have come as a light into the world, so that everyone who believes in Me would not remain in darkness.

JOHN 12:46 HCSB

The Bible says that you are "the light that gives light to the world." The Bible also says that you should live in a way that lets other people understand what it means to be a follower of Jesus.

What kind of light have you been giving off? Hopefully, you've been a good example for everybody to see. Why? Because the world needs all the light it can get, and that includes your light, too!

The old familiar hymn begins, "What a friend we have in Jesus...." No truer words were ever penned. Jesus is the sovereign friend and ultimate Savior of mankind. Christ showed enduring love for you by willingly sacrificing His own life so that you might have eternal life. As a response to His sacrifice, you should love Him, praise Him, and share His message of salvation with your neighbors and with the world.

Do you seek to be an extreme follower of Christ? Then you must let your light shine . . . today and every day.

Demonstrating Our Love

For this is the love of God, that we keep His commandments. And His commandments are not burdensome.

1 JOHN 5:3 NKJV

How can we demonstrate our love for God? By accepting His Son as our personal Savior and by placing Christ squarely at the center of our lives and our hearts. Jesus said that if we are to love Him, we must obey His commandments (John 14:15). Thus, our obedience to the Master is an expression of our love for Him.

In Ephesians 2:10 we read, "For we are His workmanship, created in Christ Jesus for good works." (NKJV). These words are instructive: We are not saved by good works, but for good works. Good works are not the root, but rather the fruit of our salvation.

Today, let the fruits of your stewardship be a clear demonstration of your love for Christ. When you do, your good heart will bring forth many good things for yourself and for God. Christ has given you spiritual abundance and eternal life. You, in turn, owe Him good treasure from a single obedient heart: yours.

Being Patient with Yourself

Rejoice in hope; be patient in affliction; be persistent in prayer.

ROMANS 12:12 HCSB

Being patient with other people can be difficult. But sometimes, we find it even more difficult to be patient with ourselves. We have high expectations and lofty goals. We want to accomplish things now, not later. And, of course, we want our lives to unfold according to our own timetables, not God's.

Throughout the Bible, we are instructed that patience is the companion of wisdom. Proverbs 16:32 teaches us that "Patience is better than strength" (NCV). And, in 1 Peter 5:6, we are told to "humble yourselves under the mighty hand of God, that He may exalt you in due time" (NKJV).

God's message, then, is clear: we must be patient with all people, beginning with that particular person who stares back at us each time we gaze into the mirror.

All things pass. Patience attains all it strives for.

ST. TERESA OF AVILA

Pause and Praise

And those who have reason to be thankful should continually sing praises to the Lord.

JAMES 5:13 NLT

Because we have been saved by God's only Son, we must never lose hope in the priceless gifts of eternal love and eternal life. And, because we are so richly blessed, we must approach our Heavenly Father with reverence and thanksgiving.

Sometimes, in our rush "to get things done," we simply don't stop long enough to pause and thank our Creator for the countless blessings He has bestowed upon us. But when we slow down and express our gratitude to the One who made us, we enrich our own lives and the lives of those around us.

Thanksgiving should become a habit, a regular part of our daily routines. God has blessed us beyond measure, and we owe Him everything, including our eternal praise. Let us praise Him today, tomorrow, and throughout eternity.

Who Rules Your Heart?

Give to the Lord the glory due His name; bring an offering, and come into His courts.

PSALM 96:8 NKJV

Who rules your heart? Is it God, or is it something else? Do you give God your firstfruits or your last? Have you given Christ your heart, your soul, your talents, your time, and your testimony? Or are you giving Him little more than a few hours each Sunday morning?

In the book of Exodus, God warns that we should place no gods before Him. Yet all too often, we place our Lord in second, third, or fourth place as we worship the gods of pride, greed, power, or personal gratification. When we unwittingly place possessions or relationships above our love for the Creator, we must seek His forgiveness and repent from our disobedience.

Does God rule your heart? Make certain that the honest answer to this question is a resounding yes. In the life of every righteous believer, God comes first. And that's precisely the place that He deserves in your heart.

Your Questions, His Answers

Our God forever and ever . . . will guide us until death.
PSALM 48:14 NASB

When you have a question that you simply can't answer, whom do you ask? When you face a difficult decision, to whom do you turn for counsel? To friends? To mentors? To family members? Or do you turn first to the Ultimate source of wisdom? The answers to life's Big Questions start with God and with the teachings of His Holy Word.

God's wisdom stands forever. God's Word is a light for every generation. Make it your light as well. Use the Bible as a compass for the next stage of your life's journey. Use it as the yardstick by which your behavior is measured. And as you carefully consult the pages of God's Word, prayerfully ask Him to reveal the wisdom that you need. When you take your concerns to God, He will not turn you away; He will, instead, offer answers that are tested and true. Your job is to ask, to listen, and to trust.

When there is perplexity there is always guidance—not always at the moment we ask, but in good time, which is God's time. There is no need to fret and stew.

ELISABETH ELLIOT

Self-Acceptance

You're blessed when you're content with just who you are—
no more, no less. That's the moment you find yourselves
proud owners of everything that can't be bought.

MATTHEW 5:5 MSG

Being patient with other people can be difficult.
But sometimes, we find it even more difficult to
be patient with ourselves. We have high expectations
and lofty goals. We want to receive God's blessings now,
not later. And, of course, we want our lives to unfold
according to our own wishes and our own timetables—
not God's. Yet throughout the Bible, we are instructed
that patience is the companion of wisdom. Proverbs
16:32 teaches us that "Patience is better than strength"
(NCV). God's message, then, is clear: we must be
patient with all people, beginning with that particular
woman who stares back at us each time we gaze into the
mirror.

The Bible affirms the importance of self-acceptance
by exhorting believers to love others as they love
themselves (Matthew 22:37-40). Furthermore, the
Bible teaches that when we genuinely open our hearts
to Him, God accepts us just as we are. And, if He
accepts us—faults and all—then who are we to believe
otherwise?

Your Growing Faith

I want you woven into a tapestry of love, in touch with everything there is to know of God. Then you will have minds confident and at rest, focused on Christ, God's great mystery.

COLOSSIANS 2:2 MSG

Your relationship with God is ongoing; it unfolds day by day, and it offers countless opportunities to grow closer to Him . . . or not. As each new day unfolds, you are confronted with a wide range of decisions: how you will behave, where you will direct your thoughts, with whom you will associate, and what you will choose to worship. These choices, along with many others like them, are yours and yours alone. How you choose determines how your relationship with God will unfold.

Are you continuing to grow in your love and knowledge of the Lord, or are you "satisfied" with the current state of your spiritual health? Hopefully, you're determined to make yourself a growing Christian. Your Savior deserves no less, and neither, by the way, do you.

Giving Thanks to the Creator

In everything give thanks; for this is the will of God in Christ Jesus for you.

1 THESSALONIANS 5:18 NKJV

Psalm 145 makes this promise: "The LORD is gracious and compassionate, slow to anger and rich in love. The LORD is good to all; he has compassion on all he has made" (8-9 NIV).

Most of us have been blessed beyond measure, but sometimes, as busy women living in a demanding world, we are sometimes slow to count our gifts and even slower to give thanks to the Giver. Our blessings include life and health, family and friends, freedom and possessions—for starters. And those blessings are multiplied when we share them with others.

As the old saying goes, "When we drink the water, we should remember the spring." May we, who have been so richly blessed, give thanks for our gifts—and may we demonstrate our gratitude by sharing them.

One reason why we don't thank God for his answer to our prayer is that frequently we don't recognize them as being answers to our prayers. We just take his bountiful supply or dramatic action for granted when it comes.

EVELYN CHRISTENSON

Whom Do You Trust?

The one who understands a matter finds success, and the one who trusts in the Lord will be happy.

PROVERBS 16:20 HCSB

Where will you place your trust today? Will you trust in the ways of the world, or will you trust in the Word and the will of your Creator?

If you aspire to do great things for God's kingdom, you will trust Him completely.

Trusting God means trusting Him in every aspect of your life. You must trust Him with your relationships. You must trust Him with your finances. You must follow His commandments and pray for His guidance. Then, you can wait patiently for God's revelations and for His blessings.

When your trust your Heavenly Father without reservation, you can rest assured: in His own fashion and in His own time, God will bless you in ways that you never could have imagined. So trust Him, and then prepare yourself for the abundance and joy that will most certainly be yours through Him.

I trust completely in God, nothing else.

ST. JOAN OF ARC

Out of Balance?

Happy is the person who finds wisdom and gains understanding.

PROVERBS 3:13 NLT

Sometimes, amid the concerns of everyday life, we lose perspective. Life seems out of balance as we confront an array of demands that sap our strength and cloud our thoughts. What's needed is a renewed faith, a fresh perspective, and God's wisdom.

Here in the 21st century, commentary is commonplace and information is everywhere. But the ultimate source of wisdom, the kind of timeless wisdom that God willingly shares with His children, is still available from a single unique source: the Holy Bible.

The wisdom of the world changes with the ever-shifting sands of public opinion. God's wisdom does not. His wisdom is eternal. It never changes. And it most certainly is the wisdom that you must use to plan your day, your life, and your eternal destiny.

Knowledge can be learned, but wisdom must be earned. Wisdom is knowledge . . . lived.

SHEILA WALSH

Don't Be Worried ... You Are Protected

But seek first his kingdom and his righteousness, and all these things will be given to you as well. Therefore do not worry about tomorrow, for tomorrow will worry about itself. Each day has enough trouble of its own.

MATTHEW 6:33-34 NIV

Because we are fallible human beings, we worry. Even though we, as Christians, have the assurance of salvation—even though we, as Christians, have the promise of God's love and protection—we find ourselves fretting over the countless details of everyday life.

If you are like most women, you may, on occasion, find yourself worrying about health, about finances, about safety, about relationships, about family, and about countless other challenges of life, some great and some small. Where is the best place to take your worries? Take them to God. Take your troubles to Him, and your fears, and your sorrows. And remember: God is trustworthy ... and you are protected.

God may say "Wait," but He never says, "Worry."

ANONYMOUS

Whom Should We Please?

*Our only goal is to please God whether we live here or there,
because we must all stand before Christ to be judged.*

2 CORINTHIANS 5:9-10 NCV

As a member in good standing of this highly competitive, 21st-century world, you know that the demands and expectations of everyday living can seem burdensome, even overwhelming at times. Keeping up with the Joneses can become a fulltime job if you let it. A better strategy, of course, is to stop trying to please the neighbors and to concentrate, instead, upon pleasing God.

Perhaps you have set your goals high; if so, congratulations! You're willing to dream big dreams, and that's a very good thing. But as you consider your life's purpose, don't allow your quest for excellence to interfere with the spiritual journey that God has planned for you.

As a believer, your instructions are clear: you must strive to please God. How do you please Him? By accepting His Son and obeying His commandments. All other concerns—including, but not limited to, keeping up with the Joneses—are of little or no importance.

Imitating Christ

For I have given you an example that you also should do just as I have done for you.

JOHN 13:15 HCSB

Every day of our lives, we make many decisions, some good, and some bad. When we live according to God's commandments, we reap bountiful rewards: abundance, hope, and peace, for starters. But, when we turn our backs upon God by disobeying Him, we bring needless suffering upon ourselves and our families.

Do you seek to walk in the footsteps of the One from Galilee, or will you choose another path? If you sincerely seek God's peace and His blessings, then you must strive to imitate God's Son.

Christ is the ultimate Savior of mankind and the personal Savior of those who believe in Him. As His servants, we should walk in His footsteps as we share His love and His message with a world that needs both.

The whole idea of belonging to Christ is to look less and less like we used to and more and more like Him.

ANGELA THOMAS

Moving Past the Past

One thing I do, forgetting those things which are behind and reaching forward to those things which are ahead, I press toward the goal for the prize of the upward call of God in Christ Jesus.

PHILIPPIANS 3:13-14 NKJV

Manmade plans are fallible; God's plans are not. Yet whenever life takes an unexpected turn, we are tempted to fall into the spiritual traps of worry, self-pity, or bitterness. God intends that we do otherwise.

The old saying is familiar: "Forgive and forget." But when we have been hurt badly, forgiveness is often difficult and forgetting is downright impossible. Since we can't forget yesterday's troubles, we should learn from them. Yesterday has much to teach us about tomorrow. We may learn from the past, but we should never live in the past. God has given each of us a glorious day: this one. And it's up to each of us to use this day as faithful stewards, not as embittered historians.

So if you're trying to forget the past, don't waste your time. Instead, try a different approach: learn to accept the past and live in the present. Then, you can focus your thoughts and your energies, not on the struggles of yesterday, but instead on the profound opportunities that God has placed before you today.

Beyond the Frustrations

But now you must also put away all the following: anger, wrath, malice, slander, and filthy language from your mouth.

COLOSSIANS 3:8 HCSB

The frustrations of everyday living can sometimes get the better of us, and we allow minor disappointments to cause us major problems. When we allow ourselves to become overly irritated by the inevitable ups and downs of life, we become overstressed, overheated, over-anxious, and just plain angry.

As singer Tina Turner once observed, "If you want to be successful, you don't have time for bitterness." And the same can be said for anger.

As the old saying goes, "Anger usually improves nothing but the arch of a cat's back." So don't allow feelings of anger or frustration to rule you life, or, for that matter, your day—your life is simply too short for that, and you deserve much better treatment than that . . . from yourself.

Anger unresolved will only bring you woe.

KAY ARTHUR

To Study or Not to Study?

Jesus answered, "It is written: 'Man does not live by bread alone, but on every word that comes from the mouth of God.'"

MATTHEW 4:4 NIV

If you really want to know God, you should read the book He wrote. It's called the Bible, and it is one of the most important tools that God uses to direct your steps and transform your life.

As you seek to build a deeper relationship with your Creator, you must decide whether God's Word will be a bright spotlight that guides your path every day or a tiny nightlight that occasionally flickers in the dark. The decision to study the Bible—or not—is yours and yours alone. But make no mistake: the way that you choose to use your Bible will have a profound impact on you and your loved ones.

Your Bible is waiting patiently on your bookshelf—now, what are you going to do about it?

The devil is not afraid of a Bible that has dust on it.

ANONYMOUS

Managing Change

The wise see danger ahead and avoid it, but fools keep going and get into trouble.

PROVERBS 27:12 NCV

There is no doubt. Your world is changing constantly. So today's question is this: How will you manage all those changes?" Will you do your best and trust God with the rest, or will you spend fruitless hours worrying about things you can't control, while doing precious little else? The answer to these simple questions will help determine the direction and quality of your life.

The best way to confront change is head-on . . . and with God by your side. The same God who created the universe will protect you if you ask Him, so ask Him—and then serve Him with willing hands and a trusting heart. When you do, you may rest assured that while the world changes moment by moment, God's love endures—unfathomable and unchanging—forever.

Live for today, but hold your hands open to tomorrow. Anticipate the future and its changes with joy. There is a seed of God's love in every event, every circumstance, every unpleasant situation in which you may find yourself.

BARBARA JOHNSON

The New You

Therefore if anyone is in Christ, he is a new creature; the old things passed away; behold, new things have come.

2 Corinthians 5:17 HCSB

Think, for a moment, about the "old" you, the person you were before you invited Christ to reign over your heart. Now, think about the "new" you, the person you have become since then. Is there a difference between the "old" you and the "new and improved" version? There should be! And that difference should be noticeable not only to you but also to others.

The Bible clearly teaches that when we welcome Christ into our hearts, we become new creations through Him. Our challenge, of course, is to behave ourselves like new creations. When we do, God fills our hearts, He blesses our endeavors, and transforms our lives . . . forever.

How do I know that Jesus has risen? Because he has risen to the throne of my own heart. I have seen him work miracles in my life, one after another, big and small. He has changed my desires; he has remodeled my thinking; he has shown me how to love the unlovable, forgive the unforgivable (including myself), and move the unmovable barriers in my path.

Liz Curtis Higgs

Facing Difficult Days

We are pressured in every way but not crushed; we are perplexed but not in despair.

2 CORINTHIANS 4:8 HCSB

All of us face difficult days. Sometimes even the most devout Christian women can become discouraged, and you are no exception. After all, you live in a world where expectations can be high and demands can be even higher.

If you find yourself enduring difficult circumstances, remember that God remains in His heaven. If you become discouraged with the direction of your day or your life, turn your thoughts and prayers to Him. He is a God of possibility, not negativity. He will guide you through your difficulties and beyond them. And then, with a renewed spirit of optimism and hope, you can thank the Giver of all things good for gifts that are simply too numerous to count.

If things are tough, remember that every flower that ever bloomed had to go through a whole lot of dirt to get there.

BARBARA JOHNSON

A Beacon of Encouragement

Encourage each other. Live in harmony and peace. Then the God of love and peace will be with you.

2 CORINTHIANS 13:11 NLT

One of the reasons that God placed you here on earth is so that you might become a beacon of encouragement to the world. As a faithful follower of the One from Galilee, you have every reason to be hopeful, and you have every reason to share your hopes with others. When you do, you will discover that hope, like other human emotions, is contagious.

As a follower of Christ, you are instructed to choose your words carefully so as to build others up through wholesome, honest encouragement (Ephesians 4:29). So look for the good in others and celebrate the good that you find. As the old saying goes, "When someone does something good, applaud—you'll make two people happy."

Once you loosen up, let yourself be who you are: the wonderful, witty woman whom God will use to encourage and uplift other people.

BARBARA JOHNSON

The Wisdom to Respect Him

The fear of the Lord is the beginning of wisdom, and the knowledge of the Holy One is understanding.

PROVERBS 9:10 NKJV

Do you have a healthy, fearful respect for God's power? If so, you are both wise and obedient. And, because you are a thoughtful believer, you also understand that genuine wisdom begins with a profound appreciation for God's limitless power.

God praises humility and punishes pride. That's why God's greatest servants will always be those humble men and women who care less for their own glory and more for God's glory. In God's kingdom, the only way to achieve greatness is to shun it. And the only way to be wise is to understand these facts: God is great; He is all-knowing; and He is all-powerful. We must respect Him, and we must humbly obey His commandments, or we must accept the consequences of our misplaced pride.

Oh, that we might all be made for love of Him who for love of us was called mad!

ST. TERESA OF AVILA

Using Our Gifts

Based on the gift they have received, everyone should use it to serve others, as good managers of the varied grace of God.

1 PETER 4:10 HCSB

How do we thank God for the gifts He has given us? By using those gifts for the glory of His kingdom.

God has given you talents and opportunities that are uniquely yours. Are you willing to use your gifts in the way that God intends? And are you willing to summon the discipline that is required to develop your talents and to hone your skills? That's precisely what God wants you to do, and that's precisely what you should desire for yourself.

As you seek to expand your talents, you will undoubtedly encounter stumbling blocks along the way, such as the fear of rejection or the fear of failure. When you do, don't stumble! Just continue to refine your skills, and offer your services to God. And when the time is right, He will use you—but it's up to you to be thoroughly prepared when He does.

God's Faithfulness

God is faithful, by whom you were called into the fellowship of His Son, Jesus Christ our Lord.

1 CORINTHIANS 1:9 NKJV

God is faithful to us even when we are not faithful to Him. God keeps His promises to us even when we stray far from His path. God offers us countless blessings, but He does not force His blessings upon us. If we are to experience His love and His grace, we must claim them for ourselves.

God is with you. Listen prayerfully to the quiet voice of your Heavenly Father. Talk with God often; seek His guidance; watch for His signs; listen to the wisdom that He shares through the reliable voice of your own conscience.

God loves you, and you deserve all the best that God has to offer. You can claim His blessings today by being faithful to Him.

It is a joy that God never abandons His children. He guides faithfully all who listen to His directions.

CORRIE TEN BOOM

A Grand Plan

I will instruct you and teach you in the way you should go;
I will guide you with My eye.

God has plans for your life that are far grander than you can imagine. But He won't force you to follow His will; to the contrary, He has given you free will, the ability to make choices and decisions on your own. The most important decision of your life is, of course, your commitment to accept Jesus Christ as your personal Lord and Savior. And once your eternal destiny is secured, you will undoubtedly ask yourself "What now, Lord?" If you earnestly seek God's will for your life, you will find it...in time.

Sometimes, God's plans are crystal clear, but other times, He may lead you through the wilderness before He delivers you to the Promised Land. So be patient, keep praying, and keep seeking His will for your life. When you do, you'll be amazed at the marvelous things that an all-powerful, all-knowing God can do.

You can believe in Jesus Christ as your Savior, make heaven and miss hell, but never realize the power that God intended for you to know in this life.

ANGELA THOMAS

The Great Commission

Go, therefore, and make disciples of all nations, baptizing them in the name of the Father and of the Son and of the Holy Spirit, teaching them to observe everything I have commanded you. And remember, I am with you always, to the end of the age.

MATTHEW 28:19-20 HCSB

Are you a bashful Christian, one who is afraid to speak up for your Savior. Do you leave it up to others to share their testimonies while you stand on the sidelines, reluctant to share yours? Too many of us are slow to obey the last commandment of the risen Christ; we don't do our best to "make disciples of all the nations."

Christ's Great Commission applies to Christians of every generation, including our own. As believers, we are commanded to share the Good News with our families, with our neighbors, and with the world. Jesus invited His disciples to become fishers of men. We, too, must accept the Savior's invitation, and we must do so today. Tomorrow may indeed be too late.

Finding Happiness and Abundance

Happy are those who fear the Lord. Yes, happy are those who delight in doing what he commands.

PSALM 112:1 NLT

Do you seek happiness, abundance, and contentment? If so, here are some things you should do: Love God and His Son; depend upon God for strength; try, to the best of your abilities, to follow God's will; and strive to obey His Holy Word. When you do these things, you'll discover that happiness goes hand-in-hand with righteousness. The happiest people are not those who rebel against God; the happiest people are those who love God and obey His commandments.

What does life have in store for you? A world full of possibilities (of course it's up to you to seize them), and God's promise of abundance (of course it's up to you to accept it). So, as you embark upon the next phase of your journey, remember to celebrate the life that God has given you. Your Creator has blessed you beyond measure. Honor Him with your prayers, your words, your deeds, and your joy.

Christ is the secret, the source, the substance, the center, and the circumference of all true and lasting gladness.

MRS. CHARLES E. COWMAN

Judging Others

Do not judge, or you too will be judged. For in the same way you judge others, you will be judged, and with the measure you use, it will be measured to you.

MATTHEW 7:1 NIV

We have all fallen short of God's commandments, and He has forgiven us. We, too, must forgive others. And, we must refrain from judging them.

Are you one of those people who finds it easy to judge others? If so, it's time to change.

God does not need (or, for that matter, want) your help. Why? Because God is perfectly capable of judging the human heart . . . while you are not.

As Christians, we are warned that to judge others is to invite fearful consequences: to the extent we judge others, so, too, will we be judged by God. Let us refrain, then, from judging our neighbors. Instead, let us forgive them and love them in the same way that God has forgiven us.

Don't judge other people more harshly than you want God to judge you.

MARIE T. FREEMAN

When Mistakes Become Lessons

The one who conceals his sins will not prosper, but whoever confesses and renounces them will find mercy.

PROVERBS 28:13 HCSB

We are imperfect women living in an imperfect world; mistakes are simply part of the price we pay for being here. But, even though mistakes are an inevitable part of life's journey, repeated mistakes should not be. When we commit the inevitable blunders of life, we must correct them, learn from them, and pray to God for the wisdom not to repeat them. And then, if we are successful, our mistakes become lessons, and our lives become adventures in growth, not stagnation.

Mistakes offer the possibility for redemption and a new start in God's kingdom. No matter what you're guilty of, God can restore your innocence.

BARBARA JOHNSON

We become a failure when we allow mistakes to take away our ability to learn, give, grow, and try again.

SUSAN LENZKES

Accepting the Past

I do not consider myself yet to have taken hold of it. But one thing I do: Forgetting what is behind and straining toward what is ahead, I press on toward the goal to win the prize for which God has called me heavenward in Christ Jesus.

PHILIPPIANS 3:13-14 NIV

When you find the courage to accept the past by forgiving all those who have injured you (including yourself), you can then look to the future with a sense of optimism and hope.

Because we are saved by a risen Christ, we can have hope for the future, no matter how troublesome our circumstances may seem. After all, God has promised that we are His throughout eternity. And, He has told us that we must place our hopes in Him.

Of course, we will face disappointments and failures while we are here on earth, but these are only temporary defeats. Of course, this world can be a place of trials and tribulations, but we are secure. God has promised us peace, joy, and eternal life. And God keeps His promises today, tomorrow, and forever.

Spiritual Traps

Why are you cast down, O my soul? And why are you disquieted within me? Hope in God; For I shall yet praise Him, The help of my countenance and my God.

PSALM 42:11 NKJV

Pessimism and Christianity don't mix. Why? Because Christians have every reason to be optimistic about life here on earth and life eternal.

Sometimes, despite our trust in God, we may fall into the spiritual traps of worry, frustration, anxiety, or sheer exhaustion, and our hearts become heavy. What's needed is plenty of rest, a large dose of perspective, and God's healing touch, but not necessarily in that order.

Today, make this promise to yourself and keep it: vow to be a hope-filled Christian. Think optimistically about your life, your profession, and your future. Trust your hopes, not your fears. Take time to celebrate God's glorious creation. And then, when you've filled your heart with hope and gladness, share your optimism with others. They'll be better for it, and so will you. But not necessarily in that order.

Attitude is the mind's paintbrush; it can color any situation.

BARBARA JOHNSON

Infinite Possibilities

All things are possible for the one who believes.

MARK 9:23 NCV

We live in a world of infinite possibilities. But sometimes, because of limited faith and limited understanding, we wrongly assume that God cannot or will not intervene in the affairs of mankind. Such assumptions are simply wrong.

Are you afraid to ask God to do big things in your life? Is your faith threadbare and worn? If so, it's time to abandon your doubts and reclaim your faith—faith in yourself, faith in your abilities, faith in your future, and faith in your Heavenly Father.

Catherine Marshall notes that, "God specializes in things thought impossible." And make no mistake: God can help you do things you never dreamed possible . . . your job is to let Him.

Unbelief keeps us living beneath the possibilities that God dreamed for our lives.

ANGELA THOMAS

When we reach the end of our abilities, God's possibilities are just beginning.

EMILIE BARNES

God Responds

Whatever you ask for in prayer, believe that you have received it, and it will be yours.

MARK 11:24 NIV

When we petition God, He responds. God's hand is not absent, and it is not distant. It is responsive.

On his second missionary journey, Paul started a small church in Thessalonica. A short time later, he penned a letter that was intended to encourage the new believers at that church. Today, almost 2,000 years later, 1 Thessalonians remains a powerful, practical guide for Christian living.

In his letter, Paul advises members of the new church to "pray without ceasing." His advice applies to Christians of every generation. When we weave the habit of prayer into the very fabric of our days, we invite God to become a partner in every aspect of our lives. When we consult God on an hourly basis, we avail ourselves of His wisdom, His strength, and His love.

Today, allow the responsive hand of God to guide you and help you. Pray without ceasing, and then rest assured: God is listening . . . and responding!

Purpose and Service

Your attitude should be the same as that of Christ Jesus . . .
taking the very nature of a servant.

PHILIPPIANS 2:5,7 NIV

The teachings of Jesus are clear: We achieve greatness through humble service. So, as you seek to discover God's purpose for your life, you may rest assured that His plan for you is centered around service to your family, to your friends, to your church, to your community, and to the world.

Today, you may feel the temptation to build yourself up in the eyes of your neighbors. Resist that temptation. Instead, serve your neighbors quietly and without fanfare. Find a need and fill it . . . humbly. Lend a helping hand and share a word of kindness . . . anonymously, for this is God's way.

As a humble servant, you will glorify yourself not before men, but before God, and that's what God intends. After all, earthly glory is fleeting: here today and soon gone. But, heavenly glory endures throughout eternity. So the choice is yours: Either you can lift yourself up here on earth and be humbled in heaven, or vice versa. Choose vice versa.

Right with God

The Good News shows how God makes people right with himself—that it begins and ends with faith. As the Scripture says, "But those who are right with God will live by trusting in him."

ROMANS 1:17 NCV

How do we live a life that is "right with God"? By accepting God's Son and obeying His commandments. Accepting Christ is a decision that we make one time; following in His footsteps requires thousands of decisions each day.

Whose steps will you follow today? Will you honor God as you strive to follow His Son? Or will you join the lockstep legion that seeks to discover happiness and fulfillment through worldly means? If you are righteous and wise, you will follow Christ. You will follow Him today and every day. You will seek to walk in His footsteps without reservation or doubt. When you do so, you will be "right with God" precisely because you are walking aright with His only begotten Son.

Holiness is not God's asking us to be "good"; it is an invitation to be "His."

LISA BEVERE

As The World Grows Louder

Be silent before the Lord and wait expectantly for Him.
PSALM 37:7 HCSB

The world seems to grow louder day by day, and our senses seem to be invaded at every turn. If we allow the distractions of a clamorous society to separate us from God's peace, we do ourselves a profound disservice. Our task, as dutiful believers, is to carve out moments of silence in a world filled with noise.

If we are to maintain righteous minds and compassionate hearts, we must take time each day for prayer and for meditation. We must make ourselves still in the presence of our Creator. We must quiet our minds and our hearts so that we might sense God's will and His love.

Has the busy pace of life robbed you of the peace that God has promised? If so, it's time to reorder your priorities and your life. Nothing is more important than the time you spend with your Heavenly Father. So be still and claim the inner peace that is found in the silent moments you spend with God.

Defining Success

If you do not stand firm in your faith, then you will not stand at all.

ISAIAH 7:9 HCSB

How do you define success? Do you define it as the accumulation of material possessions or the adulation of your neighbors? If so, you need to reorder your priorities. Genuine success has little to do with fame or fortune; it has everything to do with God's gift of love and His promise of salvation.

If you have accepted Christ as your personal Savior, you are already a towering success in the eyes of God, but there is still more that you can do. Your task—as a believer who has been touched by the Creator's grace—is to accept the spiritual abundance and peace that He offers through the person of His Son. Then, you can share the healing message of God's love and His abundance with a world that desperately needs both. When you do, you have reached the pinnacle of success.

Nothing I can do will make me special. No awards I can earn will make me a better person. The taproot of my being grows in the rich soil of the being of Christ instead of in the shifting sands of worldly accomplishment.

LESLIE WILLIAMS

Each Day a Gift

Teach us to number our days carefully so that we may develop wisdom in our hearts.

PSALM 90:12 HCSB

This day is a gift from God. How will you use it? Will you celebrate God's gifts and obey His commandments? Will you share words of encouragement and hope with all who cross your path? Will you share the Good News of the risen Christ? Will you trust in the Father and praise His glorious handiwork? The answer to these questions will determine, to a surprising extent, the direction and the quality of your day.

The familiar words of Psalm 118:24 remind us of a profound yet simple truth: "This is the day which the LORD hath made; we will rejoice and be glad in it" (KJV). For Christian believers, every day begins and ends with God and His Son. Christ came to this earth to give us abundant life and eternal salvation. We give thanks to our Maker when we treasure each day and use it to the fullest.

Today, may we give thanks for this day and for the One who created it.

When Your Faith Is Tested

Blessed be the God and Father of our Lord Jesus Christ, the Father of mercies and the God of all comfort. He comforts us in all our affliction, so that we may be able to comfort those who are in any kind of affliction, through the comfort we ourselves receive from God.

2 Corinthians 1:3-4 HCSB

When the sun is shining and all is well, it is easy to have faith. But, when life takes an unexpected turn for the worse, as it will from time to time, your faith will be tested. In times of trouble and doubt, God remains faithful to you—and you must retain faith in yourself.

Social activist Jane Addams observed, "You do not know what life means when all the difficulties are removed. It's like eating a sweet dessert the first thing in the morning." And so it is with your own life.

So the next time you spot storm clouds on the horizon, remind yourself that every difficult day must come to an end . . . and when tough times are tough, tough women (like you) are tougher.

You and I need to learn to interpret our circumstances by His love, not interpret His love by our circumstances!

Anne Graham Lotz

Your Reasons to Rejoice

Keep your eyes focused on what is right, and look straight ahead to what is good.

PROVERBS 4:25 NCV

As a Christian woman, you have every reason to rejoice. God is in His heaven; Christ has risen, and dawn has broken on another day of life. But, when the demands of life seem great, you may find yourself feeling exhausted, discouraged, or both. That's when you need a fresh supply of hope . . . and God is ready, willing, and able to supply it.

The advice contained in Proverbs 4:5 is clear-cut: "Keep your eyes focused on what is right, and look straight ahead to what is good" (NCV). That's why you strive to maintain a positive, can-do attitude—an attitude that pleases God.

As you face the challenges of the coming day, use God's Word as a tool for directing your thoughts. When you do, your attitude will be pleasing to God, pleasing to your friends, and pleasing to yourself.

No matter how little we can change about our circumstances, we always have a choice about our attitude toward the situation.

VONETTE BRIGHT

Time to Celebrate

Rejoice in the Lord always. I will say it again: Rejoice!
PHILIPPIANS 4:4 HCSB

Are you living a life of agitation, consternation, or celebration? If you're a believer, it should most certainly be the latter. With Christ as your Savior, every day should be a time of celebration.

Today, celebrate the life that God has given you. Today, put a smile on your face, kind words on your lips, and a song in your heart. Be generous with your praise and free with your encouragement. And then, when you have celebrated life to the full, invite your friends to do likewise. After all, this is God's day, and He has given us clear instructions for its use. We are commanded to rejoice and be glad. So, with no further ado, let the celebration begin...

If you can forgive the person you were, accept the person you are, and believe in the person you will become, you are headed for joy. So celebrate your life.

BARBARA JOHNSON

The proper perspective creates within us a spirit of reaching outside of ourselves with joy and enthusiasm.

LUCI SWINDOLL

Love With No Limits

For I am persuaded that neither death nor life, nor angels nor principalities nor powers, nor things present nor things to come, nor height nor depth, nor any other created thing, shall be able to separate us from the love of God which is in Christ Jesus our Lord.

ROMANS 8:38-39 NKJV

God's love for us is unconditional. No matter what we have done good or bad God's love is steady and sure. Even though we are imperfect, fallible human beings, even though we have fallen far short of God's commandments, Christ loves us still. His love is perfect; it does not waver—it does not change. Our task, as believers, is to accept Christ's love and to encourage others to do likewise.

In today's troubled world, we all need the love and the peace that is found through the Son of God. Thankfully, Christ's love has no limits. We, in turn, should love Him with no limits, beginning now and ending never.

The love of Christ is a fierce thing. It can take the picture you have of yourself and burn it in the fire of his loving eyes, replacing it with a true masterpiece.

SHEILA WALSH

Your Daily Journey

Then He said to them all, "If anyone wants to come with Me, he must deny himself, take up his cross daily, and follow Me."

LUKE 9:23 HCSB

Even the most inspired women can, from time to time, find themselves running on empty. Why? Because the inevitable demands of daily life can drain us of our strength and rob us of the joy that is rightfully ours in Christ. Thankfully, God stands ready to renew our spirits, even on the darkest of days. God's Word is clear: When we genuinely lift our hearts and prayers to Him, He renews our strength.

Are you almost too weary to lift your head? Then bow it—in prayer. Offer your concerns and your needs to your Father in Heaven. He is always at your side, offering His love and His strength.

Your search to discover God's purpose for your life is not a destination; it is a journey that unfolds day by day. And, that's exactly how often you should seek direction from your Creator: one day at a time, each day followed by the next, without exception.

An early walk and talk with the Lord will last all day.

ANONYMOUS

When Faith Slips Away

Immediately the father of the child cried out and said with tears, "Lord, I believe; help my unbelief!"

MARK 9:24 NKJV

Sometimes, like Jesus' disciples, we feel threatened by the storms of life. During these moments, when we our hearts are flooded with uncertainty, we must remember that God is not simply near, He is here.

Have you ever felt your faith in God slipping away? If so, you are in good company. Even the most faithful Christians are, at times, beset by occasional bouts of discouragement and doubt. But even when you feel far removed from God, God never leaves your side. He is always with you, always willing to calm the storms of life. When you sincerely seek His presence—and when you genuinely seek to establish a deeper, more meaningful relationship with His Son—God will calm your fears, answer your prayers, and restore your soul.

We must lay our questions, frustrations, anxieties, and impotence at the feet of God and wait for His answer. And then receiving it, we must live by faith.

KAY ARTHUR

Actions Speak Louder

Because the kingdom of God is present not in talk but in power.

1 CORINTHIANS 4:20 NCV

O ur words speak, but our actions speak much more loudly. And whether we like it or not, all of us are role models. Since our friends and family members observe our actions, we are obliged to act in ways that demonstrate what it means to be a follower of Christ. As the old saying goes, "It's good to be saved and know it! But It's even better to be saved and show it!"

Today, make this promise to your God and to yourself: promise to be the kind of role model that honors your heavenly Father and His only begotten Son. When you do so, you will be an ambassador for Christ and a positive role model to a world that needs both.

Every word we speak, every action we take, has an effect on the totality of humanity. No one can escape that privilege—or that responsibility.

LAURIE BETH JONES

Forgiveness and Spiritual Growth

If anyone says, "I am living in the light," but hates a Christian brother or sister, that person is still living in darkness.

1 JOHN 2:9 NLT

Forgiveness is an exercise in spiritual growth: the more we forgive, the more we grow. Conversely, bitterness makes spiritual growth impossible: when our hearts are filled with resentment and anger, there is no room left for love.

As Christians, we can and should continue to grow in the love and the knowledge of our Savior as long as we live. When we cease to grow, either emotionally or spiritually, we do ourselves and our loved ones a profound disservice. But, if we study God's Word, if we obey His commandments, and if we live in the center of His will, we will not be "stagnant" believers; we will, instead, be growing Christians . . . and that's exactly what God wants for our lives.

In those quiet moments when we open our hearts to God, the Creator who made us keeps remaking us. He gives us direction, perspective, wisdom, and courage. And the appropriate moment to accept His spiritual gifts is always this one.

God's Comfort

Praise be to the God and Father of our Lord Jesus Christ. God is the Father who is full of mercy and all comfort. He comforts us every time we have trouble, so when others have trouble, we can comfort them with the same comfort God gives us.

2 CORINTHIANS 1:3-4 NCV

We live in a world that is, at times, a frightening place. We live in a world that is, at times, a discouraging place. We live in a world where life-changing losses can be so painful and so profound that it seems we will never recover. But with God's help, and with the help of encouraging family members and friends, we can recover.

During the darker days of life, we are wise to remember that God is with us always and that He offers us comfort, assurance, and peace—our task, of course, is to accept these gifts.

When we trust in God's promises, the world becomes a less frightening place. With God's comfort and His love in our hearts, we can tackle our problems with courage, determination, and faith.

Your Relationship with God

Unfailing love surrounds those who trust the LORD.

PSALM 32:10 NLT

St. Augustine observed, "God loves each of us as if there were only one of us." Do you believe those words? Do you seek to have an intimate, one-on-one relationship with your Heavenly Father, or are you satisfied to keep Him at a "safe" distance?

Sometimes, in the crush of our daily duties, God may seem far away, but He is not. God is everywhere we have ever been and everywhere we will ever go. He is with us night and day; He knows our thoughts and our prayers. And, when we earnestly seek Him, we will find Him because He is here, waiting patiently for us to reach out to Him.

Let us reach out to Him today and always. And let us praise Him for the glorious gifts that have transformed us today and forever. Amen.

There is no pit so deep that God's love is not deeper still.

CORRIE TEN BOOM

He Provides

The Lord is my rock and my fortress and my deliverer; the God of my strength, in whom I will trust.

2 SAMUEL 22:2-3 NKJV

As a busy woman, you know from firsthand experience that life is not always easy. But as a recipient of God's grace, you also know that you are protected by a loving Heavenly Father.

In times of trouble, God will comfort you; in times of sorrow, He will dry your tears. When you are troubled, or weak, or sorrowful, God is neither distant nor disinterested. To the contrary, God is always present and always vitally engaged in the events of your life. Reach out to Him, and build your future on the rock that cannot be shaken . . . trust in God and rely upon His provisions. He can provide everything you really need . . . and far, far more.

When you live a surrendered life, God is willing and able to provide for your every need.

CORRIE TEN BOOM

It is enough to know his promise that he will give what is good—he knows so much more about that than we do.

ELISABETH ELLIOT

Your Hope, Your Confidence

Lord, I turn my hope to You. My God, I trust in You.
PSALM 25:1-2 HCSB

The hope that the world offers is fleeting and imperfect. The hope that God offers is unchanging, unshakable, and unending. It is no wonder, then, that when we seek security from worldly sources, our hopes are often dashed. Thankfully, God has no such record of failure.

Where will you place your hopes today? Will you entrust your future to man or to God? Will you seek solace exclusively from fallible human beings, or will you place your hopes, first and foremost, in the trusting hands of your Creator? The decision is yours, and you must live with the results of the choice you make.

For thoughtful believers, hope begins with God. Period. So today, as you embark upon the next stage of your life's journey, consider the words of the Psalmist: "You are my hope; O Lord GOD, You are my confidence" (71:5 NASB). Then, place your trust in the One who cannot be shaken.

Listening to God

The one who is from God listens to God's words. This is why you don't listen, because you are not from God.

JOHN 8:47 HCSB

Sometimes God speaks loudly and clearly. More often, He speaks in a quiet voice—and if you are wise, you will be listening carefully when He does. To do so, you must carve out quiet moments each day to study His Word and sense His direction.

Can you quiet yourself long enough to listen to your conscience? Are you attuned to the subtle guidance of your intuition? Are you willing to pray sincerely and then to wait quietly for God's response? Hopefully so. Usually God refrains from sending His messages on stone tablets or city billboards. More often, He communicates in subtler ways. If you sincerely desire to hear His voice, you must listen carefully, and you must do so in the silent corners of your quiet, willing heart.

When I am constantly running there is no time for being. When there is no time for being there is no time for listening.

MADELEINE L'ENGLE

Optimistic Christianity

Make me to hear joy and gladness.

PSALM 51:8 KJV

Are you an optimistic, hopeful, enthusiastic Christian? You should be. After all, as a believer, you have every reason to be optimistic about life here on earth and life eternal. As C. H. Spurgeon observed, "Our hope in Christ for the future is the mainstream of our joy." But sometimes, you may find yourself pulled down by the inevitable demands and worries of life-here-on-earth. If you find yourself discouraged, exhausted, or both, then it's time to take your concerns to God. When you do, He will lift your spirits and renew your strength.

Today, make this promise to yourself and keep it: vow to be a hope-filled Christian. Think optimistically about your life, your profession, your family, and your future. Trust your hopes, not your fears. Take time to celebrate God's glorious creation. And then, when you've filled your heart with hope and gladness, share your optimism with others. They'll be better for it, and so will you.

Full Confidence

May the God of hope fill you with all joy and peace as you trust in him, so that you may overflow with hope by the power of the Holy Spirit.

ROMANS 15:13 NIV

Sometimes, peace can be a scarce commodity in a demanding, 21st-century world. How, then, can we find the peace that we so desperately desire? By slowing down, by keeping problems in perspective, by counting our blessings, and by trusting God.

Dorothy Harrison Pentecost writes, "Peace is full confidence that God is Who He says He is and that He will keep every promise in His Word."

And Beth Moore advises, "Prayer guards hearts and minds and causes God to bring peace out of chaos."

So today, as you journey out into the chaos of the world, bring God's peace with you. And remember: the chaos is temporary, but God's peace is not.

To know God as He really is—in His essential nature and character—is to arrive at a citadel of peace that circumstances may storm, but can never capture.

CATHERINE MARSHALL

Praising His Marvelous Works

Enter into His gates with thanksgiving, and into His courts with praise. Be thankful to Him, and bless His name. For the Lord is good; His mercy is everlasting, and His truth endures to all generations.

PSALM 100:4-5 NKJV

In the Hebrew version of the Old Testament, the title of the book of Psalms is translated "hymns of praise," and with good reason. Much of the book is a breathtakingly beautiful celebration of God's power, God's love, and God's creation. The psalmist writes, "Let everything that breathes praise the Lord. Hallelujah!" (150:6 HCSB).

As Christians, we should continually praise God for all that He has done and all that He will do. His works are marvelous, His gifts are beyond understanding, and His love endures forever.

Do you sincerely desire to be a worthy servant of the One who has given you eternal love and eternal life? Then praise Him. And don't just praise Him on Sunday morning. Praise Him all day long, every day, for as long as you live . . . and then for all eternity.

First Things First

First pay attention to me, and then relax. Now you can take it easy—you're in good hands.

PROVERBS 1:33 MSG

"First things first." These words are easy to speak but hard to put into practice. For busy women living in a demanding world, placing first things first can be difficult indeed. Why? Because so many people are expecting so many things from us!

If you're having trouble prioritizing your day, perhaps you've been trying to organize your life according to your own plans, not God's. A better strategy, of course, is to take your daily obligations and place them in the hands of the One who created you. To do so, you must prioritize your day according to God's commandments, and you must seek His will and His wisdom in all matters. Then, you can face the day with the assurance that the same God who created our universe out of nothingness will help you place first things first in your own life.

Do you feel overwhelmed or confused? Turn the concerns of this day over to God—prayerfully, earnestly, and often. Then listen for His answer . . . and trust the answer He gives.

He Renews

Finally, be strengthened by the Lord and by His vast strength.

EPHESIANS 6:10 HCSB

God's Word is clear: When we genuinely lift our hearts and prayers to Him, He renews our strength. Are you almost too weary to lift your head? Then bow it. Offer your concerns and your fears to your Father in Heaven. He is always at your side, offering His love and His strength.

Are you troubled or anxious? Take your anxieties to God in prayer. Are you weak or worried? Delve deeply into God's Holy Word and sense His presence in the quiet moments of the early morning. Are you spiritually exhausted? Call upon fellow believers to support you, and call upon Christ to renew your spirit and your life. Your Savior will not let you down. To the contrary, He will lift you up when you ask Him to do so. So what, dear friend, are you waiting for?

In those desperate times when we feel like we don't have an ounce of strength, He will gently pick up our heads so that our eyes can behold something—something that will keep His hope alive in us.

KATHY TROCCOLI

Respecting Your Talents

Every good gift and every perfect gift is from above, and cometh down from the Father of lights.

JAMES 1:17 KJV

Do you place a high value on your talents, your time, your capabilities and your opportunities? If so, congratulations. But if you've acquired the insidious habit of devaluing your time, your work, or yourself, it's now time for a change.

Pearl Bailey correctly observed, "The first and worst of all frauds is to cheat one's self. All sin is easy after that."

If you've been squandering opportunities or selling yourself short, it's time to rethink the way that you think about yourself and your opportunities. No one can seize those opportunities for you, and no one can build up your self-confidence if you're unwilling to believe in yourself. So if you've been talking yourself down, stop. You deserve better. And if you don't give yourself healthy respect, who will?

Give yourself a gift today: be present with yourself. God is. Enjoy your own personality. God does.

BARBARA JOHNSON

The Journey Toward Spiritual Maturity

For this reason also, since the day we heard this, we haven't stopped praying for you. We are asking that you may be filled with the knowledge of His will in all wisdom and spiritual understanding.

COLOSSIANS 1:9 HCSB

The journey toward spiritual maturity lasts a lifetime: As Christians, we can and should continue to grow in the love and the knowledge of our Savior as long as we live. Norman Vincent Peale had simple advice for believers of all ages: "Ask the God who made you to keep remaking you." That advice, of course, is perfectly sound, but too often ignored.

When we cease to grow, either emotionally or spiritually, we do ourselves and our families a profound disservice. But, if we study God's Word, if we obey His commandments, and if we live in the center of His will, we will not be "stagnant" believers; we will, instead, be growing Christians.

In those quiet moments when we open our hearts to God, the Creator who made us keeps remaking us. He gives us direction, perspective, wisdom, and courage. And, the appropriate moment to accept His spiritual gifts is always this one.

Thank Him Now

Our prayers for you are always spilling over into thanksgivings. We can't quit thanking God our Father and Jesus our Messiah for you!

COLOSSIANS 1:3 MSG

Sometimes, life-here-on-earth can be complicated, demanding, and frustrating. When the demands of life leave us rushing from place to place with scarcely a moment to spare, we may fail to pause and thank our Creator for the countless blessings He bestows upon us. But, whenever we neglect to give proper thanks to the Giver of all things good, we suffer because of our misplaced priorities.

As believers who have been saved by a risen Christ, we are blessed beyond human comprehension. We who have been given so much should make thanksgiving a habit, a regular part of our daily routines. Of course, God's gifts are too numerous to count, but we should attempt to count them nonetheless. We owe our Heavenly Father everything, including our eternal praise . . . starting right now.

Let's thank God for allowing us to experience troubles that drive us closer to Him.

SHIRLEY DOBSON

He Cares for You

Trust in the LORD with all your heart; do not depend on your own understanding. Seek his will in all you do, and he will direct your paths.

PROVERBS 3:5-6 NLT

Open your Bible to its center, and you'll find the Book of Psalms. In it are some of the most beautiful words ever translated into the English language, with none more beautiful than the 23rd Psalm. David describes God as being like a shepherd who cares for His flock. No wonder these verses have provided comfort and hope for generations of believers.

On occasion, you will confront circumstances that trouble you to the very core of your soul. When you are afraid, trust in God. When you are worried, turn your concerns over to Him. When you are anxious, be still and listen for the quiet assurance of God's promises. And then, place your life in His hands. He is your Shepherd today and throughout eternity. Trust the Shepherd.

The more we learn to receive and depend upon His grace in deepening measure, the less anxious we will be about what the future holds.

CYNTHIA HEALD

Seeking His Wisdom

Wisdom is the principal thing; therefore get wisdom. And in all your getting, get understanding.

PROVERBS 4:7 NKJV

D o you seek the wisdom that only God can give? If so, ask Him for it! If you ask God for guidance, He will not withhold it. If you petition Him sincerely, and if you genuinely seek to form a relationship with Him, your Heavenly Father will guide your steps and enlighten your heart. But be forewarned: You will not acquire God's wisdom without obeying His commandments. Why? Because God's wisdom is more than just a collection of thoughts; it is, first and foremost, a way of life.

Wisdom is as wisdom does. So if you sincerely seek God's wisdom, don't be satisfied to learn something; make up your mind to become something. And then, as you allow God to remake you in the image of His Son, you will most surely become wise.

Knowledge can be found in books or in school. Wisdom, on the other hand, starts with God . . . and ends there.

MARIE T. FREEMAN

Worship Him

But an hour is coming, and is now here, when the true worshipers will worship the Father in spirit and truth. Yes, the Father wants such people to worship Him. God is Spirit, and those who worship Him must worship in spirit and truth.

John 4:23-24 HCSB

Where do we worship? In our hearts or in our church? The answer is both. As Christians who have been saved by a loving, compassionate Creator, we are compelled not only to worship the Creator in our hearts but also to worship Him in the presence of fellow believers.

We live in a world that is teeming with temptations and distractions—a world where good and evil struggle in a constant battle to win our hearts and souls. Our challenge, of course, is to ensure that we cast our lot on the side of God. One way to ensure that we do so is by the practice of regular, purposeful worship with our families. When we worship God faithfully and fervently, we are blessed.

God Sees

Do you think I am trying to make people accept me? No, God is the One I am trying to please. Am I trying to please people? If I still wanted to please people, I would not be a servant of Christ.

GALATIANS 1:10 NCV

The world sees you as you appear to be; God sees you as you really are . . . He sees your heart, and He understands your intentions. The opinions of others should be relatively unimportant to you; however, God's view of you—His understanding of your actions, your thoughts, and your motivations—should be vitally important.

Few things in life are more futile than "keeping up appearances" for the sake of neighbors. What is important, of course, is pleasing your Father in heaven. You please Him when your intentions are pure and your actions are just.

Are you trying to keep up with the Joneses? Don't even try . . . you've got better things to do—far better things—like pleasing your Father in heaven.

Many people never receive God's best for them because they are addicted to the approval of others.

JOYCE MEYER

Beyond Jealousy

Where jealousy and selfishness are, there will be confusion and every kind of evil.

JAMES 3:14 NCV

Are you too wise to be consumed with feelings of jealousy? Hopefully so. After all, Jesus clearly taught us to love our neighbors, not to envy them. But sometimes, despite our best intentions, we fall prey to feelings of resentfulness, jealousy, bitterness, and envy. Why? Because we are human, and because we live in a world that places great importance on material possessions (possessions which, by the way, are totally unimportant to God).

The next time you feel pangs of envy invading your thoughts, remind yourself of two things: 1. Envy is a sin, and 2. God has already showered you with so many blessings that if you're a thoughtful, thankful believer, you have no right to ever be envious of any other person on earth.

Faith Tip:
You can be envious, or you can be happy,
but you can't be both. Envy and happiness can't
live at the same time in the same brain.

Acceptance Today

I have learned to be content whatever the circumstances.

PHILIPPIANS 4:11 NIV

Are you embittered by a personal tragedy that you did not deserve and cannot understand? If so, it's time to accept the unchangeable past and to have faith in the promise of tomorrow. It's time to trust God completely—and it's time to reclaim the peace—His peace—that can and should be yours.

On occasion, you will be confronted with situations that you simply don't understand. But God does. And He has a reason for everything that He does.

God doesn't explain Himself in ways that we, as mortals with limited insight and clouded vision, can comprehend. So, instead of understanding every aspect of God's unfolding plan for our lives and our universe, we must be satisfied to trust Him completely. We cannot know God's motivations, nor can we understand His actions. We can, however, trust Him, and we must.

Ultimately things work out best for those who make the best of the way things work out.

BARBARA JOHNSON

Where to Take Your Troubles

Be anxious for nothing, but in everything by prayer and supplication, with thanksgiving, let your requests be made known to God.

PHILIPPIANS 4:6 NKJV

Sometimes, the world seems to shift beneath our feet. From time to time, all of us face adversity, discouragement, or disappointment. And, throughout life, we must all endure life-changing personal losses that leave us anxiously struggling for breath. When we do, God stands ready to protect us.

The Bible instructs us to, "Be strong and courageous, and do the work. Don't be afraid or discouraged, for the Lord God, my God, is with you. He won't leave you or forsake you" (1 Chronicles 28:20 HCSB). When we are troubled, we must call upon God, and in time He will heal us.

Are you anxious? Take those anxieties to God. Are you troubled? Take your troubles to Him. Does your future seem uncertain? Place your trust in the One who is forever faithful.

God's Roadmap

Every word of God is flawless; he is a shield to those who take refuge in him.

PROVERBS 30:5 NIV

God's Word is unlike any other book. The Bible is a roadmap for life here on earth and for life eternal. As Christians, we are called upon to study God's Holy Word, to trust its promises, to follow its commandments, and to share its Good News with the world.

As women who seek to follow in the footsteps of the One from Galilee, we must study the Bible and meditate upon its meaning for our lives. Otherwise, we deprive ourselves of a priceless gift from our Creator. God's Holy Word is, indeed, a transforming, life-changing, one-of-a-kind treasure. And, a passing acquaintance with the Good Book is insufficient for Christians who seek to obey God's Word and to understand His will.

The Reference Point for the Christian is the Bible. All values, judgments, and attitudes must be gauged in relationship to this Reference Point.

RUTH BELL GRAHAM

How Character Is Built

We also have joy with our troubles, because we know that these troubles produce patience. And patience produces character, and character produces hope.

ROMANS 5:3-4 NCV

Beth Moore correctly observed, "Those who walk in truth walk in liberty." Godly men and women agree. As believers in Christ, we must seek to live each day with discipline, honesty, and faith. When we do, at least two things happen: integrity becomes a habit, and God blesses us because of our obedience to Him. Living a life of integrity isn't always the easiest way, but it is always the right way . . . and God clearly intends that it should be our way, too.

Character isn't built overnight; it is built slowly over a lifetime. It is the sum of every sensible choice, every honorable decision, and every honest word. It is forged on the anvil of sincerity and polished by the virtue of fairness. Character is a precious thing—preserve yours at all costs.

Often, our character is at greater risk in prosperity than in adversity.

BETH MOORE

Obedience and Contentment

Praise the Lord! Happy are those who respect the Lord,
who want what he commands.

PSALM 112:1 NCV

When we conduct ourselves in ways that are opposed to God's commandments, we rob ourselves of God's peace. When we fall prey to the temptations and distractions of our irreverent age, we rob ourselves of God's blessings. When we become preoccupied with material possessions or personal status, we forfeit the contentment that is rightfully ours in Christ.

Where can we find the kind of contentment that Paul describes in Philippians 4:11? Is it a result of wealth, or power, or fame? Hardly. Genuine contentment is a gift from God to those who follow His commandments and accept His Son. It is a gift that must be discovered and rediscovered throughout life. It is a gift that we claim when we allow Christ to dwell at the center of our lives.

If we know we have pleased God, contentment will be our consolation, for what pleases God will please us.

KAY ARTHUR

Dealing with Difficult People

Bad temper is contagious—don't get infected.

PROVERBS 22:25 MSG

Face it: sometimes people can be difficult to deal with . . . very, very difficult. When other people are unkind to you, you may be tempted to strike back, either verbally or in some other way. Resist that temptation. Instead, remember that God corrects other people's behaviors in His own way, and He doesn't need your help (even if you're totally convinced that He does).

So when other people behave cruelly, foolishly, or impulsively—as they will from time to time—don't respond in kind. Instead, speak up for yourself as politely as you can, and walk away. Then, forgive everybody as quickly as you can and leave the rest up to God.

You don't have to attend every argument you're invited to!

ANONYMOUS

...God loves these people too, just because they're unattractive or warped in their thinking doesn't mean the Lord doesn't love them.

RUTH BELL GRAHAM

Celebrating Others

Let us think about each other and help each other to show love and do good deeds.

HEBREWS 10:24 NCV

Do you delight in the victories of others? You should. Each day provides countless opportunities to encourage others and to praise their good works. When you do so, you not only spread seeds of joy and happiness, you also obey the commandments of God's Holy Word.

Life is a team sport, and all of us need occasional pats on the back from our teammates. As Christians, we are called upon to spread the Good News of Christ, and we are also called to spread a message of encouragement and hope to the world.

Today, let us be cheerful Christians with smiles on our faces and encouraging words on our lips. By blessing others, we also bless ourselves, and, at the same time, we do honor to the One who gave His life for us.

One of the ways God refills us after failure is through the blessing of Christian fellowship. Just experiencing the joy of simple activities shared with other children of God can have a healing effect on us.

ANNE GRAHAM LOTZ

Fellowship and Hope

I want their hearts to be encouraged and joined together in love, so that they may have all the riches of assured understanding, and have the knowledge of God's mystery—Christ.

COLOSSIANS 2:2 HCSB

Every believer—including you—needs to be part of a community of faith. Your association with fellow Christians should be uplifting, enlightening, encouraging, and consistent.

Are you an active member of your fellowship? Are you a builder of bridges inside the four walls of your church and outside it? Do you contribute to God's glory by contributing your time and your talents to a close-knit band of hope-filled believers? Hopefully so. The fellowship of believers is intended to be a powerful tool for spreading God's Good News and uplifting His children. And God intends for you to be a fully contributing member of that fellowship. Your intentions should be the same.

Be united with other Christians. A wall with loose bricks is not good. The bricks must be cemented together.

CORRIE TEN BOOM

Cultivating God's Gifts

I remind you to fan into flame the gift of God.

2 TIMOTHY 1:6 NIV

All women possess special gifts and talents; you are no exception. But, your gift is no guarantee of success; it must be cultivated and nurtured; otherwise, it will go unused . . . and God's gift to you will be squandered. Today, accept this challenge: value the talent that God has given you, nourish it, make it grow, and share it with the world. After all, the best way to say "Thank You" for God's gift is to use it.

It is the definition of joy to be able to offer back to God the essence of what he's placed in you, be that creativity or a love of ideas or a compassionate heart or the gift of hospitality.

PAULA RINEHART

The splendor of the rose and the whiteness of the lily do not rob the little violet of its scent nor the daisy of its simple charm. If every tiny flower wanted to be a rose, spring would lose its loveliness.

THERESE OF LISIEUX

Always Faithful

Let us hold on to the confession of our hope without wavering, for He who promised is faithful.

HEBREWS 10:23 HCSB

The Bible makes it perfectly clear: the heart of God is always faithful. The faithfulness of God does not mean we, His children, are freed from life's problems and tragedies. It means that God will preserve us in our difficulties, not from our difficulties.

God's faithfulness is made clear in the beautiful words of Psalm 23:4: "Yea, though I walk through the valley of the shadow of death, I will fear no evil: for thou art with me; thy rod and thy staff they comfort me" (KJV). God does not exempt us the valleys of life, but neither does He ask us to walk alone. He is always there.

God's heart is faithful. He's faithful to His people; He is faithful to His Word; and He is faithful to you. Paul writes in 1 Corinthians 1:9, "God is faithful, by whom you were called into the fellowship of His Son, Jesus Christ our Lord" (NKJV). God has a faithful heart. Trust Him, and take comfort in the unerring promises and the never-ending faithfulness of your Lord.

His Surprising Plans

But as it is written in the Scriptures: "No one has ever seen this, and no one has ever heard about it. No one has ever imagined what God has prepared for those who love him."

1 CORINTHIANS 2:9 NCV

God has big plans for your life, wonderful, surprising plans ... but He won't force those plans upon you. To the contrary, He has given you free will, the ability to make decisions on your own. Now, it's up to you to make those decisions wisely.

If you seek to live in accordance with God's plan for your life, you will study His Word, you will be attentive to His instructions, and you will be watchful for His signs. You will associate with fellow believers who, by their words and actions, will encourage your spiritual growth. You will assiduously avoid those two terrible temptations: the temptation to sin and the temptation squander time. And finally, you will listen carefully, even reverently, to the conscience that God has placed in your heart.

God intends to use you in wonderful, unexpected ways if you let Him. Let Him. When you do, you'll be thoroughly surprised by the creativity and the beauty of His plans.

Close to the Brokenhearted

I am the Lord who heals you.

EXODUS 15:26 NCV

In time, tragedy visits all those who live long and love deeply. When our friends or family members encounter life-shattering events, we struggle to find words that might offer them comfort and support. But finding the right words can be difficult, if not impossible. Sometimes, all that we can do is to be with our loved ones and to pray for them, trusting that God will do the rest.

Thankfully, God promises that He is "close to the brokenhearted" (Psalm 34:18 NIV). In times of intense sadness, we must turn to Him, and we must encourage our friends and family members to do likewise. When we do so, our Father comforts us and, in time, He heals us.

In heaven, we will see that nothing, absolutely nothing, was wasted, and that every tear counted and every cry was heard.

JONI EARECKSON TADA

Holiness Before Happiness

If they serve Him obediently, they will end their days in prosperity and their years in happiness.

JOB 36:11 HCSB

Because you are an imperfect human being, you are not "perfectly" happy—and that's perfectly okay with God. He is far less concerned with your happiness than He is with your holiness.

God continuously reveals Himself in everyday life, but He does not do so in order to make you contented; He does so in order to lead you to His Son. So don't be overly concerned with your current level of happiness: it will change. Be more concerned with the current state of your relationship with Christ: He does not change. And because your Savior transcends time and space, you can be comforted in the knowledge that in the end, His joy will become your joy . . . for all eternity.

A joyful heart is like a sunshine of God's love, the hope of eternal happiness, a burning flame of God.... And if we pray, we will become that sunshine of God's love-- in our own home, the place where we live, and in the world at large.

MOTHER TERESA

Kindness Now

God has chosen you and made you his holy people. He loves you. So always do these things: Show mercy to others, be kind, humble, gentle, and patient.

COLOSSIANS 3:12 NCV

Christ showed His love for us by willingly sacrificing His own life so that we might have eternal life: "But God demonstrates his own love for us in this: While we were still sinners, Christ died for us" (Romans 5:8 NIV). We, as Christ's followers, are challenged to share His love with kind words on our lips and praise in our hearts.

Just as Christ has been—and will always be—the ultimate friend to His flock, so should we be Christlike in the kindness and generosity that we show toward others, especially those who are most in need.

When we walk each day with Jesus—and obey the commandments found in God's Holy Word—we become worthy ambassadors for Christ. When we share the love of Christ, we share a priceless gift with the world. As His servants, we must do no less.

All kindness and good deeds, we must keep silent. The result will be an inner reservoir of personality power.

CATHERINE MARSHALL

The Wisdom of Moderation

Moderation is better than muscle, self-control better than political power.

PROVERBS 16:32 MSG

Moderation and wisdom are traveling companions. If we are wise, we must learn to temper our appetites, our desires, and our impulses. When we do, we are blessed, in part, because God has created a world in which temperance is rewarded and intemperance is inevitably punished.

Would you like to improve your life? Then harness your appetites and restrain your impulses. Moderation is difficult, of course; it is especially difficult in a prosperous society such as ours. But the rewards of moderation are numerous and long-lasting. Claim those rewards today.

No one can force you to moderate your appetites. The decision to live temperately (and wisely) is yours and yours alone. And so are the consequences.

Contentment has a way of quieting insatiable desires.

MARY HUNT

At Peace with the Past

Abundant peace belongs to those who love Your instruction; nothing makes them stumble.

PSALM 119:165 HCSB

Peace and bitterness are mutually exclusive. So, if you are mired in the quicksand of regret, it's time to plan your escape. How can you do so? By accepting the past.

The world holds few if any rewards for those who remain angrily focused upon the injustices of yesterday. Still, the act of forgiveness is difficult for all but the most saintly men and women. Being frail, fallible, imperfect human beings, most of us are quick to anger, quick to blame, slow to forgive, and even slower to forget. Yet as Christians, we are commanded to forgive others, just as we, too, have been forgiven.

If you have not yet made peace with the past, it's now time to declare an end to all hostilities. When you do so, you can then learn to live quite contentedly in a much more appropriate time period: this one.

We can't just put our pasts behind us. We've got to put our pasts in front of God.

BETH MOORE

The Plan for Your Life

The plans of hard-working people earn a profit, but those who act too quickly become poor.

PROVERBS 21:5 NCV

Perhaps you have a clearly defined plan for the future, but even if you don't, rest assured that God does. God's has a definite plan for every aspect of your life. Your challenge is straightforward: to sincerely pray for God's guidance, and to obediently follow the guidance you receive.

If you're burdened by the demands of everyday life here in the 21st century, you are not alone. Life is difficult at times, and uncertain. But of this you can be sure: God has a plan for you and yours. He will communicate His plans using the Holy Spirit, His Holy Word, and your own conscience. So listen to God's voice and be watchful for His signs: He will send you messages every day of your life, including this one. Your job is to listen, to learn, to trust, and to act.

God has plans—not problems—for our lives. Before she died in the concentration camp in Ravensbruck, my sister Betsie said to me, "Corrie, your whole life has been a training for the work you are doing here in prison—and for the work you will do afterward."

CORRIE TEN BOOM

Your Potential

Have faith in the Lord your God, and you will stand strong. Have faith in his prophets, and you will succeed.

2 CHRONICLES 20:20 NCV

Do you expect your future to be bright? Are you willing to dream king-sized dreams . . . and are you willing to work diligently to make those dreams happen? Hopefully so—after all, God promises that we can do "all things" through Him. Yet most of us live far below our potential. We take half measures; we dream small dreams; we waste precious time and energy on the distractions of the world. But God has other plans for us.

In her diary, Anne Frank wrote, "The good news is that you really don't know how great you can be, how much you can love, what you can accomplish, and what your potential is." These words apply to you. You possess great potential, potential that you must use or forfeit. And the time to fulfill that potential is now.

Everyone has inside himself a piece of good news! The good news is that you really don't know how great you can be, how much you can live, what you can accomplish, and what your potential is.

ANNE FRANK

The Power of Prayer

Don't worry about anything, but in everything, through prayer and petition with thanksgiving, let your requests be made known to God.

"The power of prayer": these words are so familiar, yet sometimes we forget what they mean. Prayer is a powerful tool for communicating with our Creator; it is an opportunity to commune with the Giver of all things good. Prayer helps us find strength for today and hope for the future. Prayer is not a thing to be taken lightly or to be used infrequently.

Is prayer an integral part of your daily life, or is it a hit-or-miss habit? Do you "pray without ceasing," or is your prayer life an afterthought?

The quality of your spiritual life will be in direct proportion to the quality of your prayer life. Prayer changes things, and it changes you. Today, instead of worrying about your next decision, ask God to lead the way. Don't limit your prayers to meals or to bedtime. Pray constantly about things great and small. God is listening, and He wants to hear from you now.

There will be no power in our lives apart from prayer.

ANGELA THOMAS

Your Next Move

It is better to take refuge in the Lord than to trust in man.

PSALM 118:8 HCSB

Does God have a plan for your life? Of course He does! Every day of your life, He is trying to lead you along a path of His choosing . . . but He won't force you to follow. God has given you free will, the opportunity to make decisions for yourself. The choices are yours: either you will choose to obey His Word and seek His will, or you will choose to follow a different path.

Today, as you carve out a few quiet moments to commune with your Heavenly Father, ask Him to renew your sense of purpose. God's plans for you may be far bigger than you imagine, but He may be waiting for you to make the next move—so today, make that move prayerfully, faithfully, and expectantly. And after you've made your move, trust God to make His.

The only Person who has ever brought sustained power and purpose into my life is the living person of God. The only words that keep making sense are His words. The only way that always stands is His way.

ANGELA THOMAS

Play It Safe?

*Cast your burden upon the Lord and He will sustain you;
He will never allow the righteous to be shaken.*

PSALM 55:22 NASB

As we consider the uncertainties of the future, we are confronted with a powerful temptation: the temptation to "play it safe." Unwilling to move mountains, we fret over molehills. Unwilling to entertain great hopes for the tomorrow, we focus on the unfairness of the today. Unwilling to trust God completely, we take timid half-steps when God intends that we make giant leaps.

Today, ask God for the courage to step beyond the boundaries of your doubts. Ask Him to guide you to a place where you can realize your full potential—a place where you are freed from the fear of failure. Ask Him to do His part, and promise Him that you will do your part. Don't ask Him to lead you to a "safe" place; ask Him to lead you to the "right" place . . . and remember: those two places are seldom the same.

To be vulnerable is to voluntarily place yourself, for the sake of a larger purpose, in a situation that could bring pain.

PAULA RINEHART

Simplicity

Whoever becomes simple and elemental again, like this child, will rank high in God's kingdom.

MATTHEW 18:4 MSG

You live in a world where simplicity is in short supply. Think for a moment about the complexity of your every-day life and compare it to the lives of your ancestors. Certainly, you are the beneficiary of many technological innovations, but those innovations have a price: in all likelihood, your world is highly complex.

Unless you take firm control of your time and your life, you may be overwhelmed by an ever-increasing tidal wave of complexity that threatens your happiness. But your Heavenly Father understands the joy of living simply, and so should you. So do yourself a favor: keep your life as simple as possible. Simplicity is, indeed, genius. By simplifying your life, you are destined to improve it.

These are three things that God especially loves: True faith with a pure heart, a simple life with a religious spirit, and openhandedness inspired by charity.

ITA OF KILLEEDY

He Preserves Us

He will wipe away every tear from their eyes. Death will exist no longer; grief, crying, and pain will exist no longer, because the previous things have passed away.

REVELATION 21:4 HCSB

Women of every generation have experienced adversity, and this generation is no different. But, today's women face challenges that previous generations could have scarcely imagined. Thankfully, although the world continues to change, God's love remains constant. And, He remains ready to comfort us and strengthen us whenever we turn to Him.

Paula Rinehart advised, "If you want to know real joy in life, then be willing to let pain tutor your soul." These words remind us that when we face up to suffering, we grow spiritually and emotionally.

When we encounter troubles, of whatever kind, we should call upon God, and in time, He will heal us. And until He does, we may be comforted in the knowledge that we never suffer alone.

Night Is Coming

I must work the works of Him who sent Me while it is day; the night is coming when no one can work.

JOHN 9:4 NKJV

The words of John 9:4 remind us that "night is coming" for all of us. But until then, God gives us each day and fills it to the brim with possibilities. The day is presented to us fresh and clean at midnight, free of charge, but we must beware: Today is a nonrenewable resource—once it's gone, it's gone forever. Our responsibility, of course, is to use this day in the service of God's will and in accordance with His commandments.

Today, treasure the time that God has given you. And search for the hidden possibilities that God has placed along your path. This day is a priceless gift from your Creator, so use it joyfully and productively. And encourage others to do likewise. After all, night is coming when no one can work . . .

God gave you this glorious day. Don't disappoint Him. Use it for His glory.

MARIE T. FREEMAN

A God of Infinite Possibilities

We are troubled on every side, yet not distressed; we are perplexed, but not in despair....

2 CORINTHIANS 4:8 KJV

As we travel the roads of life, all of us are confronted with streets that seem to be dead ends. When we do, we may become discouraged. After all, we live in a society where expectations can be high and demands even higher.

If you find yourself enduring difficult circumstances, remember that God remains in His heaven. If you become discouraged with the direction of your day or your life, turn your thoughts and prayers to Him. He is a God of possibility, not negativity. He will guide you through your difficulties and beyond them. And then, with a renewed spirit of optimism and hope, you can thank the Giver of all things good for gifts that are simply too profound to fully understand and for treasures that are too numerous to count.

He did not say: You will not be troubled—you will not be tempted—you will not be distressed. But He did say: You will not be overcome.

JULIANA OF NORWICH

The Balancing Act

Come to Me, all you who labor and are heavy laden, and I will give you rest. Take My yoke upon you and learn from Me, for I am gentle and lowly in heart, and you will find rest for your souls. For My yoke is easy and My burden is light.

MATTHEW 11:28-30 NKJV

Face facts: life is a delicate balancing act, a tightrope walk with over-commitment on one side and under-commitment on the other. And it's up to each of us to walk carefully on that rope, not falling prey to pride (which causes us to attempt too much) or to fear (which causes us to attempt too little).

God's Word promises us the possibility of abundance (John 10:10). And we are far more likely to experience that abundance when we lead balanced lives.

Are you doing too much—or too little? If so, it's time to have a little chat with God. And if you listen carefully to His instructions, you strive to achieve a more balanced life, a life that's right for you and your loved ones. When you do, everybody wins.

Every one of us is supposed to be a powerhouse for God, living in balance and harmony within and without.

JOYCE MEYER

The Best Day to Celebrate

Celebrate God all day, every day. I mean, revel in him!
PHILIPPIANS 4:4 MSG

What is the best day to celebrate life? This one! Today and every day should be a day of prayer and celebration as we consider the Good News of God's free gift: salvation through Jesus Christ.

What do you expect from the day ahead? Are you expecting God to do wonderful things, or are you living beneath a cloud of apprehension and doubt? The familiar words of Psalm 118:24 remind us of a profound yet simple truth: "This is the day which the LORD hath made" (KJV). Our duty, as believers, is to rejoice in God's marvelous creation.

For Christians, every day begins and ends with God and His Son. Christ came to this earth to give us abundant life and eternal salvation. We give thanks to our Maker when we treasure each day. May we use our time here on earth to serve God, to celebrate His marvelous gifts, and to share His Good News with the world.

Feed the Church of God

Take heed therefore unto yourselves, and to all the flock, over the which the Holy Ghost hath made you overseers, to feed the church of God.

ACTS 20:28 KJV

In the Book of Acts, Luke reminds us to "feed the church of God." As Christians who have been saved by a loving, compassionate Creator, we are compelled not only to worship Him in our hearts but also to worship Him in the presence of fellow believers.

The church belongs to God; it is His just as certainly as we are His. When we help build God's church, we bear witness to the changes that He has made in our lives.

Today and every day, let us worship God with grateful hearts and helping hands as we support the church that He has created. Let us witness to our friends, to our families, and to the world. When we do so, we bless others and we are blessed by the One who sent His Son to die so that we might have eternal life.

Churches do not lack great scholars and great minds. They lack men and women who can and will be channels of the power of God.

CORRIE TEN BOOM

Difficult Decisions

Now if any of you lacks wisdom, he should ask God, who gives to all generously and without criticizing, and it will be given to him.

JAMES 1:5 HCSB

Are you facing a difficult decision, a troubling circumstance, or a powerful temptation? If so, it's time to step back, to stop focusing on the world, and to focus, instead, on the will of your Father in heaven. The world will often lead you astray, but God will not. His counsel leads you to Himself, which, of course, is the path He has always intended for you to take.

Everyday living is an exercise in decision-making. Today and every day you must make choices: choices about what you will do, what you will worship, and how you will think. When in doubt, make choices that you sincerely believe will bring you to a closer relationship with God. And if you're uncertain of your next step, pray about it. When you do, answers will come. And you may rest assured that when God answers prayer, His answers are the right ones for you.

Faith is a decision. It is not a deduction from the facts around us.

ELISABETH ELLIOT

Big Dreams

*With God's power working in us, God can do much, much
more than anything we can ask or imagine.*

EPHESIANS 3:20 NCV

She was born in rural Mississippi and lived with
her grandmother in a house that had no indoor
plumbing. She made it to college in Nashville, where
she got her start in television. Over time, she moved to
the top of her profession, and today, her show, *Oprah*, is
an unparralled hit.

When questioned about her journey to the top,
Oprah said, "God can dream a bigger dream than we
can dream for ourselves." She was right. So try Oprah's
formula: increase the size of your dreams. Because the
Good Lord's plan for each of us is big, very big. But it's
up to us to accept the part, to step up on stage and to
perform.

The future lies all before us. Shall it only be a slight
advance upon what we usually do? Ought it not to be
a bound, a leap forward to altitudes of endeavor and
success undreamed of before?

ANNIE ARMSTRONG

Faith for the Future

For we walk by faith, not by sight.

2 CORINTHIANS 5:7 NKJV

The first element of a successful life is faith: faith in God, faith in His Son, and faith in His promises. If we place our lives in God's hands, our faith is rewarded in ways that we—as human beings with clouded vision and limited understanding—can scarcely comprehend. But, if we seek to rely solely upon our own resources, or if we seek earthly success outside the boundaries of God's commandments, we reap a bitter harvest for ourselves and for our loved ones.

Do you desire the abundance and success that God has promised? Then trust Him today and every day that you live. Trust Him with every aspect of your life. Trust His promises, and trust in the saving grace of His only begotten Son. Then, when you have entrusted your future to the Giver of all things good, rest assured that your future is secure, not only for today, but also for all eternity.

Fear knocked at the door. Faith answered. No one was there.

ANONYMOUS

Forgiveness Is Liberating

Those who show mercy to others are happy, because God will show mercy to them.

MATTHEW 5:7 NCV

Bitterness is a form of self-punishment; forgiveness is a means of self-liberation. Bitterness focuses on the injustices of the past; forgiveness focuses on the blessings of the present and the opportunities of the future. Bitterness is an emotion that destroys you; forgiveness is a decision that empowers you. Bitterness is folly; forgiveness is wisdom.

Sometimes, amid the demands of daily life, we lose perspective. Life seems out of balance, and the pressures of everyday living seem overwhelming. What's needed is a fresh perspective, a restored sense of balance . . . and God's wisdom.

If we call upon the Lord and seek to see the world through His eyes, He will give us guidance, wisdom and perspective. When we make God's priorities our priorities, He will lead us according to His plan and according to His commandments. When we study God's Word, we are reminded that God's reality is the ultimate reality. May we live—and forgive—accordingly.

His Will and Ours

Blessed are those servants, whom the lord when he cometh shall find watching....

LUKE 12:37 KJV

God has will, and so do we. He gave us the power to make choices for ourselves, and He created a world in which those choices have consequences. The ultimate choice that we face, of course, is what to do about God. We can cast our lot with Him by choosing Jesus Christ as our personal Savior, or not. The choice is ours alone.

We also face thousands of small choices that make up the fabric of daily life. When we align those choices with God's commandments, and when we align our lives with God's will, we receive His abundance, His peace, and His joy. But when we struggle against God's will for our lives, we reap a bitter harvest indeed.

Today, you'll face thousands of small choices; as you do, use God's Word as your guide. And, as you face the ultimate choice, place God's Son and God's will and God's love at the center of your life. You'll discover that God's plan is far grander than any you could have imagined.

Your Response to His Love

*This is how much God loved the world: He gave his Son,
his one and only Son. And this is why: so that no one need
by destroyed; by believing in him anyone can have a whole
and lasting life.*

JOHN 3:16 MSG

God's love for you is deeper and more profound than you can fathom. And now, precisely because you are a wondrous creation treasured by God, a question presents itself: What will you do in response to God's love? Will you ignore it or embrace it? Will you return it or neglect it? The decision, of course, is yours and yours alone.

When you embrace God's love, you are forever changed. When you embrace God's love, you feel differently about yourself, your neighbors, and your world. When you embrace God's love, you share His message and you obey His commandments.

When you accept the Father's grace and share His love, you are blessed here on earth and throughout all eternity. Accept His love today.

As the sun shines on all things on earth in the same way, yet as if each is separate, that is how God's love is for each of us: the same yet unique.

ST. THÉRÈSE OF LISIEUX

God's Sovereignty

Can you solve the mysteries of God? Can you discover everything there is to know about the Almighty? Such knowledge is higher than the heavens—but who are you? It is deeper than the underworld—what can you know in comparison to him? It is broader than the earth and wider than the sea.

JOB 11:7-9 NLT

God is sovereign. He reigns over the entire universe and He reigns over your little corner of that universe. Your challenge is to recognize God's sovereignty and live in accordance with His commandments. Sometimes, of course, this is easier said than done.

Your Heavenly Father may not always reveal Himself as quickly (or as clearly) as you would like. But rest assured: God is in control, God is here, and God intends to use you in wonderful, unexpected ways. He desires to lead you along a path of His choosing. Your challenge is to watch, to listen, to learn . . . and to follow.

To know that God rules over all—that there are no accidents in life, that no tactic of Satan or man can ever thwart the will of God—brings divine comfort.

KAY ARTHUR

The Self-fulfilling Prophecy

But as for me, I will hope continually, and will praise You yet more and more.

PSALM 71:14 NASB

The self-fulfilling prophecy is alive, well, and living at your house. If you trust God and have faith for the future, your optimistic beliefs will give you direction and motivation. That's one reason that you should never lose hope, but certainly not the only reason. The primary reason that you, as a believer, should never lose hope, is because of God's unfailing promises.

Your thoughts have the power to lift you up or to hold you down. When you acquire the habit of hopeful thinking, you will have acquired a powerful tool for improving your life. So if you find yourself falling into the spiritual traps of worry and discouragement, seek the healing touch of Jesus and the encouraging words of fellow Christians. And if you fall into the terrible habit of negative thinking, think again. After all, God's Word teaches us that Christ can overcome every difficulty (John 16:33). And when God makes a promise, He keeps it.

Loving God

Love the LORD your God with all your heart and with all your soul and with all your strength.

DEUTERONOMY 6:5 NIV

If you want to know God in a more meaningful way, you'll need to open up your heart and let Him in.

C. S. Lewis observed, "A person's spiritual health is exactly proportional to his love for God." If you hope to receive a full measure of God's spiritual blessings, you must invite your Creator to rule over your heart. When you honor God in this way, His love expands to fill your heart and bless your life.

St. Augustine wrote, "I love you, Lord, not doubtingly, but with absolute certainty. Your Word beat upon my heart until I fell in love with you, and now the universe and everything in it tells me to love you."

Today, open your heart to the Father. And let your obedience be a fitting response to His never-ending love.

You have been made by God, for God, and apart from Him there will always be emptiness in your soul.

ANGELA THOMAS

Expecting God's Blessings

My cup runs over. Surely goodness and mercy shall follow me all the days of my life; and I will dwell in the house of the Lord forever.

PSALM 23:5-6 NKJV

As you look at the landscape of your life, do you see opportunities, possibilities, and blessings, or do you focus, instead, upon the more negative scenery? Do you spend more time counting your blessings or your misfortunes? If you've acquired the unfortunate habit of focusing too intently upon the negative aspects of life, then your spiritual vision is in need of correction.

Today is yet another gift from God, and it presents yet another opportunity to thank Him for His gifts . . . or not. And if you're wise, you'll give thanks early and often.

The way that you choose to view the scenery around you will have a profound impact on the quality, the tone, and the direction of your life. The more you focus on the beauty that surrounds you, the more beautiful your own life becomes.

Developing a positive attitude means working continually to find what is uplifting and encouraging.

BARBARA JOHNSON

His Peace

But now in Christ Jesus you who once were far off have been brought near by the blood of Christ. For He Himself is our peace.

EPHESIANS 2:13-14 NKJV

On many occasions, our outer struggles are simply manifestations of the inner conflicts that we feel when we stray from God's path. What's needed is a refresher course in God's promise of peace. The beautiful words of John 14:27 remind us that Jesus offers peace, not as the world gives, but as He alone gives: "Peace I leave with you. My peace I give to you. I do not give to you as the world gives. Your heart must not be troubled or fearful" (HCSB).

As believers, our challenge is straightforward: we should welcome Christ's peace into our hearts and then, as best we can, share His peace with our neighbors.

Today, as a gift to yourself, to your family, and to your friends, invite Christ to preside over every aspect of your life. It's the best way to live and the surest path to peace . . . today and forever.

Praising the Savior

At the name of Jesus every knee should bow, of those in heaven, and of those on earth, and of those under the earth, and that every tongue should confess that Jesus Christ is Lord, to the glory of God the Father.

PHILIPPIANS 2:10-11 NKJV

The words by Fanny Crosby are familiar: "This is my story, this is my song, praising my Savior, all the day long." As believers who have been saved by the blood of a risen Christ, we must do exactly as the song instructs: We must praise our Savior time and time again throughout the day. Worship and praise should be a part of everything we do. Otherwise, we quickly lose perspective as we fall prey to the demands of everyday life.

Do you sincerely desire to be a worthy servant of the One who has given you eternal love and eternal life? Then praise Him for who He is and for what He has done for you. And don't just praise Him on Sunday morning. Praise Him all day long, every day, for as long as you live . . . and then for all eternity.

God is worthy of our praise and is pleased when we come before Him with thanksgiving.

SHIRLEY DOBSON

Working for the Harvest

So I saw that the best thing people can do is to enjoy their work, because that is all they have. No one can help another person see what will happen in the future.

ECCLESIASTES 3:22 NCV

Once the season for planting is upon us, the time to plant seeds is when we make time to plant seeds. And when it comes to planting God's seeds in the soil of eternity, the only certain time that we have is now. Yet because we are fallible human beings with limited vision and misplaced priorities, we may be tempted to delay.

If we hope to reap a bountiful harvest for God, for our families, and for ourselves, we must plant now by defeating a dreaded human frailty: the habit of procrastination. Procrastination often results from our shortsighted attempts to postpone temporary discomfort.

A far better strategy is this: Whatever "it" is, do it now. When you do, you won't have to worry about "it" later.

Faith Tip:
Today, think about that things
you've been putting off . . . and why.

A New Sense of Joy

Take My yoke upon you and learn from Me, because I am gentle and humble in heart, and you will find rest for your souls. For My yoke is easy and My burden is light.

MATTHEW 11:29-30 HCSB

Even the most inspired Christian women can, from time to time, find themselves running on empty. The demands of daily life can drain us of our strength and rob us of the joy that is rightfully ours in Christ. Are you tired or troubled? Turn your heart toward God in prayer. Are you weak or worried? Take the time—or, more accurately, make the time—to delve deeply into God's Holy Word. Are you spiritually depleted? Call upon fellow believers to support you, and call upon Christ to renew your spirit and your life. When you do, you'll discover that the Creator of the universe stands always ready and always able to create a new sense of wonderment and joy in you.

When we reach the end of our strength, wisdom, and personal resources, we enter into the beginning of his glorious provisions.

PATSY CLAIRMONT

Disciplining Yourself

Therefore, get your minds ready for action, being self-disciplined, and set your hope completely on the grace to be brought to you at the revelation of Jesus Christ. As obedient children, do not be conformed to the desires of your former ignorance but, as the One who called you is holy, you also are to be holy in all your conduct.

1 PETER 1:13-15 HCSB

God's Word is clear: as believers, we are called to lead lives of discipline, diligence, moderation, and maturity. But the world often tempts us to do otherwise. Everywhere we turn, or so it seems, we are faced with powerful temptations to behave in undisciplined, ungodly ways—but God has far better plans for our days and for our lives.

God's Word instructs us to be disciplined in our thoughts and our actions; God's Word warns us against the dangers of impulsive behavior. God's Word teaches us that diligence is rewarded and laziness is not.

Do you seek to reap the rewards that God offers those who lead disciplined lives? If so, then you must learn to discipline yourself . . . before God does.

Your Journey Continues

I've told you these things for a purpose: that my joy might be your joy, and your joy wholly mature.

JOHN 15:11 MSG

Complete spiritual maturity is never achieved in a day, or a in year, or even in a lifetime. The journey toward spiritual maturity is an ongoing process that continues, day by day, throughout every stage of life. Every stage of life has its opportunities and its challenges, and if we're wise, we continue to seek God's guidance as each new chapter of life unfolds. Norman Vincent Peale advised: "Ask the God who made you to keep remaking you." That counsel is perfectly sound, but easy to ignore.

When we cease to grow, either emotionally or spiritually, we do ourselves a profound disservice. But, if we focus our thoughts—and attune our hearts—to the will of God, we will make each day another stage in the spiritual journey . . . and that's precisely what God intends for us to do.

I'm not what I want to be. I'm not what I'm going to be. But, thank God, I'm not what I was!

GLORIA GAITHER

Too Busy to Give Thanks?

Enter into His gates with thanksgiving, and into His courts with praise. Be thankful to Him, and bless His name. For the Lord is good; His mercy is everlasting, and His truth endures to all generations.

PSALM 100:4-5 NKJV

Life has a way of constantly coming at us. Days, hours, and moments are filled with urgent demands requiring our immediate attention.

When the demands of life leave us rushing from place to place with scarcely a moment to spare, we may fail to pause and thank our Creator for His gifts. But, whenever we neglect to give proper thanks to the Father, we suffer because of our misplaced priorities.

Today, make a special effort to give thanks to the Creator for His blessings. His love for you is eternal, as are His gifts. And it's never too soon—or too late—to offer Him thanks.

If you can't seem to find time for God, then you're simply too busy for your own good. God is never too busy for you, and you should never be too busy for Him.

MARIE T. FREEMAN

Trust Him

And God, in his mighty power, will protect you until you receive this salvation, because you are trusting him.

1 PETER 1:5 NLT

Sometimes the future seems bright, and sometimes it does not. Yet even when we cannot see the possibilities of tomorrow, God can. As believers, our challenge is to trust an uncertain future to an all-powerful God.

When we trust God, we should trust Him without reservation. We should steel ourselves against the inevitable disappointments of the day, secure in the knowledge that our Heavenly Father has a plan for the future that only He can see.

Can you place your future into the hands of a loving and all-knowing God? Can you live amid the uncertainties of today, knowing that God has dominion over all your tomorrows? If you can, you are wise and you are blessed. When you trust God with everything you are and everything you have, He will bless you now and forever.

Faith is nothing more or less than actively trusting God.

CATHERINE MARSHALL

Wisdom for You and Yours

Does not wisdom call out? Does not understanding raise her voice? On the heights along the way, where the paths meet, she takes her stand.

PROVERBS 8:1-2 NIV

Do you seek wisdom for yourself and for your family? Of course you do. But, as a thoughtful woman living in a society that is filled with temptations and distractions, you know that it's all too easy for parents and children alike to stray far from the source of the ultimate wisdom: God's Holy Word.

When you commit yourself to daily study of God's Word—and when you live according to His commandments—you will become wise . . . in time. But don't expect to open your Bible today and be wise tomorrow. Acquiring wisdom takes time.

Today and every day, as a way of understanding God's plan for your life, you should study His Word and live by it. When you do, you will accumulate a storehouse of wisdom that will enrich your own life and the lives of your family members, your friends, and the world.

Seek wisdom. It's out there.

SHEILA WALSH

How Will You Worship?

For it is written, "You shall worship the Lord your God, and Him only you shall serve."

MATTHEW 4:10 NKJV

All of mankind is engaged in the practice of worship. Some choose to worship God and, as a result, reap the joy that He intends for His children. Others distance themselves from God by worshiping such things as earthly possessions or personal gratification . . . . and when they do so, they suffer.

Today, as one way of worshipping God, make every aspect of your life a cause for celebration and praise. Praise God for the blessings and opportunities that He has given you, and live according to the beautiful words found in the 5th chapter of 1 Thessalonians: "Rejoice evermore. Pray without ceasing. In every thing give thanks: for this is the will of God in Christ Jesus concerning you" (16-18 KJV).

God deserves your worship, your prayers, your praise, and your thanks. And you deserve the joy that is yours when you worship Him with your prayers, with your deeds, and with your life.

The Need to Persevere

Patient endurance is what you need now, so you will continue to do God's will. Then you will receive all that he has promised.

HEBREWS 10:36 NLT

If you've led a perfect life with absolutely no foul ups, blunders, mistakes, or flops, you can skip this page. But if you're like the rest of us, you know that occasional disappointments and failures are an inevitable part of life. These setbacks are simply the price of growing up and learning about life. But even when you experience bitter disappointments, you must never lose faith.

The Bible teaches us to persevere: "For you need endurance, so that after you have done God's will, you may receive what was promised." These reassuring words from Hebrews 10:36 (HCSB) remind us that when we persevere, we will eventually receive that which God has promised. What's required of us is perseverance, not perfection.

When we encounter the inevitable difficulties of life, God stands ready to protect us. And, while we are waiting for God's plans to unfold, we can be comforted in the knowledge that our Creator can overcome any obstacle, even if we cannot.

Our Best Friend

No one has greater love than this, that someone would lay down his life for his friends.

JOHN 15:13 HCSB

Who's the best friend this world has ever had? Jesus, of course. And when you form a life-changing relationship with Him, He'll will be your best friend, too . . . your friend forever.

Jesus has offered to share the gifts of everlasting life and everlasting love with the world and with you. If you make mistakes, He'll stand by you. If you fall short of His commandments, He'll still love you. If you feel lonely or worried, He can touch your heart and lift your spirits.

Jesus wants you to enjoy a happy, healthy, abundant life. He wants you to walk with Him and to share His Good News. You can do it. And with a friend like Jesus, you will.

Blessed assurance, Jesus is mine! O what a foretaste of glory divine!

FANNY CROSBY

His Abundance

I have come that they may have life, and that they may have it more abundantly.

JOHN 10:10 NKJV

The Bible gives us hope—as Christians we can enjoy lives filled with abundance.

But what, exactly, did Jesus mean when, in John 10:10, He promised "life . . . more abundantly"? Was He referring to material possessions or financial wealth? Hardly. Jesus offers a different kind of abundance: a spiritual richness that extends beyond the temporal boundaries of this world.

Is material abundance part of God's plan for our lives? Perhaps. But in every circumstance of life, during times of wealth or times of want, God will provide us what we need if we trust Him (Matthew 6). May we, as believers, claim the riches of Christ Jesus every day that we live, and may we share His blessings with all who cross our path.

God is the giver, and we are the receivers. And His richest gifts are bestowed not upon those who do the greatest things, but upon those who accept His abundance and His grace.

HANNAH WHITALL SMITH

Asking for Wisdom

If you need wisdom—if you want to know what God wants you to do—ask him, and he will gladly tell you. He will not resent your asking.

JAMES 1:5 NLT

How often do you ask God for His help and His wisdom? Occasionally? Intermittently? Whenever you experience a crisis? Hopefully not. Hopefully, you've acquired the habit of asking for God's assistance early and often. And hopefully, you have learned to seek His guidance in every aspect of your life.

The Bible promises that God will guide you if you let Him. Your job is to let Him. But sometimes, you will be tempted to do otherwise. Sometimes, you'll be tempted to go along with the crowd; other times, you'll be tempted to do things your way, not God's way. When you feel those temptations, resist them.

God has promised that when you ask for His help, He will not withhold it. So ask. Ask Him to meet the needs of your day. Ask Him to lead you, to protect you, and to correct you. And trust the answers He gives.

God stands at the door and waits. When you knock, He opens. When you ask, He answers. Your task is to seek His guidance prayerfully, confidently, and often.

A Spiritual Sickness

But if you harbor bitter envy and selfish ambition in your hearts, do not boast about it or deny the truth. Such "wisdom" does not come down from heaven but is earthly, unspiritual, of the devil.

JAMES 3:14-16 NIV

Bitterness is a spiritual sickness. It will consume your soul; it is dangerous to your emotional health. It can destroy you if you let it . . . so don't let it!

If you are caught up in intense feelings of anger or resentment, you know all too well the destructive power of these emotions. How can you rid yourself of these feelings? First, you must prayerfully ask God to cleanse your heart. Then, you must learn to catch yourself whenever thoughts of bitterness or hatred begin to attack you. Your challenge is this: You must learn to resist negative thoughts before they hijack your emotions.

Matthew 5:22 teaches us that if we judge our brothers and sisters, we, too, will be subject to judgement. Let us refrain, then, from judging our neighbors. Instead, let us forgive them and love them, while leaving their judgement to a far more capable authority: the One who sits on His throne in heaven.

Receiving His Joy

I have spoken these things to you so that My joy may be in you and your joy may be complete.

JOHN 15:11 HCSB

Few things in life are more sad, or, for that matter, more absurd, than a grumpy Christian. Christ promises us lives of abundance and joy, but He does not force His joy upon us. We must claim His joy for ourselves, and when we do, Jesus, in turn, fills our spirits with His power and His love.

How can we receive from Christ the joy that is rightfully ours? By giving Him what is rightfully His: our hearts and our souls.

When we earnestly commit ourselves to the Savior of mankind, when we place Jesus at the center of our lives and trust Him as our personal Savior, He will transform us, not just for today, but for all eternity. Then we, as God's children, can share Christ's joy and His message with a world that needs both.

When we bring sunshine into the lives of others, we're warmed by it ourselves. When we spill a little happiness, it splashes on us.

BARBARA JOHNSON

When Life Is Difficult

Be strong and courageous. Do not be terrified; do not be discouraged, for the LORD your God will be with you wherever you go.

JOSHUA 1:9 NIV

Life-here-on-earth can be difficult and discouraging at times. During our darkest moments, God offers us strength and courage if we turn our hearts and our prayers to Him.

As believing Christians, we have every reason to live courageously. After all, the ultimate battle has already been fought and won on the cross at Calvary. But sometimes, because we are imperfect human beings who possess imperfect faith, we fall prey to fear and doubt. The answer to our fears, of course, is God.

The next time you find your courage tested to the limit, remember that God is as near as your next breath. He is your shield and your strength; He is your protector and your deliverer. Call upon Him in your hour of need and then be comforted. Whatever your challenge, whatever your trouble, God can handle it . . . and will!

God knows that the strength that comes from wrestling with our fear will give us wings to fly.

PAULA RINEHART

God Rewards Discipline

Apply your heart to discipline And your ears to words of knowledge.

PROVERBS 23:12 NASB

God's Word reminds us again and again that our Creator expects us to lead disciplined lives. God doesn't reward laziness, misbehavior, or apathy. To the contrary, He expects believers to behave with dignity and discipline.

We live in a world in which leisure is glorified and indifference is often glamorized. But God has other plans. He did not create us for lives of mediocrity; He created us for far greater things.

Life's greatest rewards seldom fall into our laps; to the contrary, our greatest accomplishments usually require lots of work, which is perfectly fine with God. After all, He knows that we're up to the task, and He has big plans for us; may we, as disciplined believers, always be worthy of those plans.

While chastening is always difficult, if we look to God for the lesson we should learn, we will see spiritual fruit.

VONETTE BRIGHT

Strength for Today

Those who hope in the LORD will renew their strength.
They will soar on wings like eagles; they will run and not
grow weary, they will walk and not be faint.

ISAIAH 40:31 NIV

All of us have moments when we feel drained. All of us suffer through difficult days, trying times, and perplexing periods of our lives. Thankfully, God stands ready and willing to give us comfort and strength if we turn to Him.

Burning the candle at both ends is tempting but potentially destructive. Instead, we should place first things first by saying no to the things that we simply don't have the time or the energy to do. As we establish our priorities, we should turn to God and to His Holy Word for guidance.

If you're a woman with too many demands and too few hours in which to meet them, don't fret. Instead, focus upon God and upon His love for you. Then, ask Him for the wisdom to prioritize your life and the strength to fulfill your responsibilities. God will give you the energy to do the most important things on today's to-do list...if you ask Him. So ask Him.

Is Christ the Focus?

I do not consider myself to have taken hold of it. But one thing I do: forgetting what is behind and reaching forward to what is ahead, I pursue as my goal the prize promised by God's heavenly call in Christ Jesus.

PHILIPPIANS 3:13-14 HCSB

Is Christ the focus of your life? Are you fired with enthusiasm for Him? Are you an energized Christian who allows God's Son to reign over every aspect of your day? Make no mistake: that's exactly what God intends for you to do.

God has given you the gift of eternal life through His Son. In response to God's priceless gift, you are instructed to focus your thoughts, your prayers, and your energies upon God and His only begotten Son. To do so, you must resist the subtle yet powerful temptation to become a "spiritual dabbler."

A person who dabbles in the Christian faith is unwilling to place God in His rightful place: above all other things. Resist that temptation; make God the cornerstone and the touchstone of your life. When you do, He will give you all the strength and wisdom you need to live victoriously for Him.

God Can Handle It

God—His way is perfect; the word of the Lord is pure. He is a shield to all who take refuge in Him.

PSALM 18:30 HCSB

In 1967, a diving accident left Joni Eareckson Tada a quadriplegic. But she didn't give up. Unable to use her hands, she taught herself to paint fine art by holding a brush between her teeth. Then, the determined Mrs. Tada began writing. To date, she's completed over thirty books, and her ministry, Joni and Friends, touches the lives of millions.

Jesus said, "In this world you will have trouble. But take heart! I have overcome the world." So the next time you face a difficult day or an unexpected challenge, remember Joni's journey. If she could meet her challenges, so can you. So take heart, trust, and remember that no problem is too big for God.

When considering the size of your problems, there are two categories that you should never worry about: the problems that are small enough for you to handle, and the ones that aren't too big for God to handle.

MARIE T. FREEMAN

The Ultimate Gift

Thanks be to God for his indescribable gift!

2 CORINTHIANS 9:15 NIV

Christ died on the cross so that we might have eternal life. This gift, freely given from God's only Son, is the priceless possession of everyone who accepts Him as Lord and Savior.

Thankfully, God's grace is not an earthly reward for righteous behavior; it is, instead, a blessed spiritual gift. When we accept Christ into our hearts, we are saved by His grace. The familiar words from the book of Ephesians make God's promise perfectly clear: "For it is by grace you have been saved, through faith—and this not from yourselves, it is the gift of God—not by works, so that no one can boast" (2:8-9 NIV).

God's grace is the ultimate gift, and we owe Him our eternal gratitude. Our Heavenly Father is waiting patiently for each of us to accept His Son and receive His grace. Let us accept that gift today so that we might enjoy God's presence now and throughout all eternity.

The grace of God runs downhill toward the ones who are emptied and vulnerable, toward the ones who admit that they struggle.

ANGELA THOMAS

What Do You Expect?

I say to myself, "The Lord is mine, so I hope in him."
LAMENTATIONS 3:24 NCV

What do you expect from the day ahead? Are you expecting God to do wonderful things, or are you living beneath a cloud of apprehension and doubt? The familiar words of Psalm 118:24 remind us of a profound yet simple truth: "This is the day which the LORD hath made; we will rejoice and be glad in it" (KJV).

For Christian believers, every day begins and ends with God's Son and God's promises. When we accept Christ into our hearts, God promises us the opportunity for earthy peace and spiritual abundance. But more importantly, God promises us the priceless gift of eternal life.

As we face the inevitable challenges of life-here-on-earth, we must arm ourselves with the promises of God's Holy Word. When we do, we can expect the best, not only for the day ahead, but also for all eternity.

The meaning of hope isn't just some flimsy wishing. It's a firm confidence in God's promises—that he will ultimately set things right.

SHEILA WALSH

Your Spiritual Journey

Dear brothers and sisters, whenever trouble comes your way, let it be an opportunity for joy. For when your faith is tested, your endurance has a chance to grow. So let it grow, for when your endurance is fully developed, you will be strong in character and ready for anything.

JAMES 1:2-4 NLT

The journey toward spiritual maturity lasts a lifetime. As Christians, we can and should continue to grow in the love and the knowledge of our Savior as long as we live. Norman Vincent Peale had the following advice for believers of all ages: "Ask the God who made you to keep remaking you." That advice, of course, is perfectly sound, but often ignored.

When we cease to grow, either emotionally or spiritually, we do ourselves a profound disservice. But, if we study God's word, if we obey His commandments, and if we live in the center of His will, we will not be "stagnant" believers; we will, instead, be growing Christians . . . and that's exactly what God wants for our lives.

Hope and Happiness

But happy are those . . . whose hope is in the LORD their God.

PSALM 146:5 NLT

Hope and happiness are traveling companions. And if you're a Christian, you have every reason to be hopeful. After all, God is good; His love endures; and He has offered you the priceless gift of eternal life. But sometimes, in life's darker moments, you may lose sight of these blessings, and when you do, it's easy to lose hope.

When a suffering woman sought healing by merely touching the hem of His cloak, Jesus replied, "Daughter, be of good comfort; thy faith hath made thee whole" (Matthew 9:22 KJV). The message to believers is clear: if we are to be made whole by God, we must live by faith.

Are you a hope-filled woman? You should be. God has promised you peace, joy, and eternal life. And, of course, God keeps His promises today, tomorrow, and forever, amen!

Where Wisdom Is Found

Only the Lord gives wisdom; he gives knowledge and understanding.

PROVERBS 2:6 NCV

If we are to grow as Christians and as women, we need both knowledge and wisdom. Knowledge is found in textbooks. Wisdom, on the other hand, is found in God's Holy Word and in the carefully-chosen words of loving parents, family members, and friends. Knowledge is an important building block in a well-lived life, and it pays rich dividends both personally and professionally. But, wisdom is even more important because it refashions not only the mind, but also the heart.

It is never enough to know about spiritual things with your mind. Mental knowledge is not the same thing as truly understanding from the center of your being, which results from experiencing and doing.

ST. TERESA OF AVILA

A big difference exists between a head full of knowledge and the words of God literally abiding in us.

BETH MOORE

Neighbors

Show family affection to one another with brotherly love. Outdo one another in showing honor. Do not lack diligence; be fervent in spirit; serve the Lord. Rejoice in hope; be patient in affliction; be persistent in prayer.

ROMANS 12:10-12 HCSB

Neighbors. We know that we are instructed to love them, and yet there's so little time...and we're so busy. No matter. As Christians, we are commanded by our Lord and Savior Jesus Christ to love our neighbors just as we love ourselves. We are not asked to love our neighbors, nor are we encouraged to do so. We are commanded to love them. Period.

This very day, you will encounter someone who needs a word of encouragement, or a pat on the back, or a helping hand, or a heartfelt prayer. And, if you don't reach out to that person, who will? If you don't take the time to understand the needs of your neighbors, who will? If you don't love your brothers and sisters, who will? So, today, look for a neighbor in need...and then do something to help. Father's orders.

My Thoughts Throughout the Year

My Thoughts Throughout the Year

My Thoughts Throughout the Year

My Thoughts Throughout the Year

_____

_____

_____

_____

_____

_____

_____

_____

_____

_____

_____

_____

_____

_____

_____

_____

_____

_____

_____

My Thoughts Throughout the Year

_____

_____

_____

_____

_____

_____

_____

_____

_____

_____

_____

_____

_____

_____

_____

_____

_____

_____

_____

_____

My Thoughts Throughout the Year

_____

_____

_____

_____

_____

_____

_____

_____

_____

_____

_____

_____

_____

_____

_____

_____

_____

_____

My Thoughts Throughout the Year

My Thoughts Throughout the Year

My Thoughts Throughout the Year

My Thoughts Throughout the Year